MARTYN LEWIS

dogs in the news

Warner Books

For my wife Liz, who will have Tamen one day

A Warner Book

First published in Great Britain in 1992
by Little, Brown and Company

This edition published by Warner in 1993

A CIP catalogue record for this book is available
from the British Library

ISBN 0 7515 0250 2

Produced by Lennard Books
Mackerye End, Harpenden, Herts AL5 5DR

Jacket photograph by Mike Daines

Designed by Cooper Wilson
in association with Forest Publication Services

Printed and bound in Great Britain by
Butler & Tanner Ltd, Frome and London

Little, Brown and Company Limited
165 Great Dover Street
London SE1 4YA

CONTENTS

INTRODUCTION

'A cat looks down on you; a dog looks up to you; and a pig considers himself your equal.' The words and wisdom of the late Ralph Wightman, gardening expert and broadcaster, sent to me by a reader gently abusing my judgment in bringing out a book on *Cats in the News* before I had written one about *dogs*. Did I not know that dogs are much more popular pets than cats – 7.4 million in Britain alone – a clear 600,000 ahead of their feline rivals? Did I not understand that dogs are far more intelligent, loyal, friendly and understanding – and much better companions too?

Well, you will, I am sure, understand that the obligation imposed on BBC newscasters to maintain a near saintly balance on all matters, prevents me taking sides in that long-running skirmish between dog and cat owners everywhere. But to prove my neutrality – to make amends for what has apparently been seen as a shamefully unfair bias towards cats – I offer this wide-ranging and affectionate look at dogs of all shapes, sizes and mental conditions who have contrived to hit the headlines around the world over the last century or so.

My last dog was a ridiculously dumb English setter, optimistically called Lassie after the alert and intelligent collie that starred in the legendary Hollywood films. *My* Lassie was no Lassie! But she *was* incredibly faithful and friendly – and we rapidly adapted our lives to her eccentricities, which included sudden attacks on wholly imaginary enemies, and swiping even quite heavy objects off coffee tables with her long, continually turbo-charged tail.

Since then, I have reluctantly concluded that I am in a phase of my life that has no room for a dog. A London postage-stamp-of-a-garden at the back, a traffic-laden road out front, and a heavily pregnant British silver tabby, currently combine to make the Lewis household a dog-free zone. Besides, any anxious canine would have big trouble finding what Americans refer to as 'a window in my diary'. I currently inhabit a world where a plaintive appeal for 'walkies', would leave me scrabbling through my diary and asking if 'Friday at 7.30 a.m. for 15 minutes would be convenient'! No self-respecting dog would tolerate that.

Yet I know that a dog would be good for my family. Experience over the last decade has shown that a wide range of people – from the sick and elderly to overworked business executives – can greatly ease any stress and tension by spending just a few minutes each day with a dog. And that judgment is reinforced by the recent careful research of Dr James Serpell of the Companion Animal Research Group at the University of Cambridge.

He spent the best part of a year studying the effects of pet ownership on human health – and a remarkable tale he has to tell. He found that new dog owners did five times more walking than they'd indulged in before their pet arrived, as well as reporting a marked reduction in minor ailments such as head-aches, backache, colds and flu. Dr Serpell also discovered that dog owners enjoyed a substantial improvement in mental health!

So, in response to all the letters from such an eminently sane group of people, I offer this unbiased, unashamed tribute to the dogs – and their owners – who have romped through a hundred years' worth of newspaper headlines. Dog lovers everywhere – this one's for you!

Martyn Lewis,
Kensington,
London W8.
June 1992

STRANGE BREEDS AND BREEDERS

Dogs that bark in the night may simply be responding to imaginary enemies or the noise of wind in the trees, but in blocks of flats and built-up areas that barking can prevent many a neighbour enjoying a good night's sleep.

Vets sought to tackle the problem by offering dog-owners an operation to 'de-bark' their pets.

In 1966, a few enterprising vets sought to tackle the problem by offering dog-owners an operation to 'de-bark' their pets. Far from pulling in business, they were enveloped in cries of outrage from dog-lovers everywhere, appalled at such a cruel adjustment of the canine vocal chords. Thankfully, the idea never took off – but it did focus attention, briefly, on an ancient and primitive breed which does not bark. The basenji – not much bigger than a fox terrier – has an appearance as neat and clean as its habits, which combine with a sharp intelligence to make it an ideal pet. Boxer-like wrinkles on its forehead give it a permanently quizzical look.

It would have good reason to look even more puzzled had it come across the two dogs presented to the famous conductor Sir Malcolm Sergeant in 1964, and passed on by him to become the London Zoo's first truly musical attraction outside its aviary. Known simply as 'singing dogs', this rare breed was discovered in New Guinea in 1964. Not that they can have been too difficult to track down – their speciality is *yodelling*. Which may have been another reason why Sir Edward Hallstrom, the Director of Sydney's Taronga Park Zoo, was so keen to find a home for them on the other side of the world!

Man's best friend across 10,000 years was once his rival – hunting for food in the last ice age. The creatures of widely differing shapes, sizes and abilities that make up some four hundred breeds of dog around the world today are descended from one species, *canis familiaris*, and can count the wolf, the coyote and the jackal as their closest relatives. Humans have intervened with more than a little selective breeding to help steer them on their way. And the evolving shapes are well charted by artists down through the ages. An early woodcut from Aldrovandus in 1637 records eight distinctive breeds, some still familiar, a few disturbingly strange by today's standards. Other dogs must have thought that too, which is why none of those strange beasts are around to disturb us today!

1884 saw *The Times* gently winding up its readers with etchings of what it called 'Chinese edible dogs', on display at the Kennel Club's Crystal Palace dog show. It went on to explain that the females, Papoose and Peridot, owned by Lady M.O. Gore and offered for sale at £500 each, were just two of the

Dogs – 17th century style.

entries in the Chinese chow chow class. Lady Gore, one presumes, would not have been amused by the speculation which followed: 'We have no precise information concerning the rule by which Chinese gastronomy is directed in selecting for human food certain varieties of dog, and rejecting others; but it is supposed that many of the lower class of people in China will readily eat any flesh of that kind. The name of 'chow chow' seems fearfully significant... '

Perhaps anxious not to risk a diplomatic incident with China, *The Times* ended by concluding that 'the Chinese epicure has a refined though peculiar taste; and some of his dishes may now be tasted at the International Health Exhibition, though,' it added reassuringly, 'none of dog flesh'.

The dog and cat market in full swing.

By 1909, London's East End was in on the act, with its flourishing dog and cat market recorded in painstaking detail for the *Illustrated London News*. Here the merely curious jostled

Baskets of pooches and pups to tempt and delight even the stoniest heart.

with potential buyers as breeders unfolded baskets of pooches and pups to tempt and delight even the stoniest heart. And who cared if the promised pedigree turned out to be less than perfect!

At least London Zoo knew what it was getting in 1956 when it welcomed two of a breed not seen in Britain for over half a century. They were dogs completely devoid of any hair. With whippet-like bodies and large upright ears, they once ran wild in Mexico, but had been in danger of becoming extinct until dog-lovers stepped in to save them. So an eight-month-old bitch called Tlape and a ten-month-old puppy, Alacran, were chosen to lead the comeback in Britain. In Mexico this breed is known as 'xoloizcuintle', enough to test even the BBC pronunciation unit. London Zoo bottled out of that, wisely preferring to label them 'rare, hairless dogs'.

A very bare Mexican puppy braves the English climate.

Not to be confused with the 'hairless hot-water bottle dog', a breed with a 3000-year pedigree. A hairy head is separated from hairy legs by a totally nude middle, but despite that, its body temperature is four degrees higher than the average pet, and becomes even warmer after meals. Hardly surprising, then, that its ancestors were once used to keep sick people warm in bed – hence the rather derogatory nickname. Properly called the Chinese crested dog, it became so unpopular that the breed died out completely in China, and in the early 1960s an elderly American lady owned the only known examples in the world. Then breeders came to appreciate that it was not only an excellent, intelligent house pet, but it didn't smell – or shed. As odourless dogs are – let's

It was not only an excellent, intelligent house pet, but it didn't smell.

face it – few and far between, it wasn't long before 'hot-water bottles' began appearing at more and more dog shows. Not all were as naked as nature intended. Owners rapidly discovered that virtually every Chinese crested litter contains at least one pup with a full body of hair. Known as 'powder puffs', they are thought to be nature's way of ensuring that even 'hot-water bottles' have someone to keep them warm!

They wouldn't stand much chance in the tough canine world of Turkey, where it is a tradition for purebred, one-week-old Anatolian Karabash sheepdog puppies to have their ears chopped off before wolves can rip them off! Needless to say, pups like

Weight check for two Chinese crested pups.

Little Fred, born in England, are in no such danger, although he may have grown up to wonder why mum, Emma, looked a little different. The only enemy their owner, Chris Emmett from Hillingdon, had to face in 1985 was the Kennel Club, which insisted on lumping all working dogs from Turkey together under the heading of 'Anatolian shepherd dogs'. Chris thought that was wrong

– and actually went to court to preserve a more precise pedigree for Little Fred and all who follow him. 'The Anatolian Karabash', insisted Chris, 'is unique'.

It was in the sixties that the photographers of Fleet Street first discovered the dog that looks like a black dishmop. No

It is a tradition for purebred, one-week-old Anatolian Karabash sheepdog puppies to have their ears chopped off before the wolves can rip them off!

matter that the puli had been a working sheepdog in Hungary, driving off foxes, wolves and bears for more than 1000 years; its appearance – or perhaps disappearance, as some wags suggested – was at least new to British readers. 20 years later, dishmop dogs got a second media outing – at Cruft's. Only this time they were white, which made them 'rare Hungarian

No wolves in England to worry Little Fred.

Facing page
*A proud mum
and a very
wrinkled baby.*

*Dishmop on the
move.*

Komondors'. Either way, they present what is delightfully understated in polite dog circles as 'a grooming challenge'. Weighing in at up to 95 pounds, they might be forgiven for having to take a permanently dim view of life.

They present what delightfully is understated in polite dog circles as 'a grooming challenge'.

A clear monopoly of furrowed brows for those contemplating a dog's life can be claimed by the rare Chinese breed, Shar-Pei – not only the most expensive dog in the world, but clearly the most wrinkled. It was 1980 before German breeders Linda and Joachim Meinberg produced the first four to be born in Europe. Two years later, Heather Liggett, from Ewell in Surrey proudly displayed some of the first British pups; and Manchester businessman Kevin Horkin must have been pretty creased up at shelling out £1500 a-piece for *his* Shar-Peis in 1985.

Big money buys oddity, rarity and pedigree. There can be few breeds that have remained as pure and unchanged as the Egyptian greyhound. Ancient sculptures of this magnificent creature, uncovered in tombs built 4,000 years ago, bear a

THERE—YOUR
SHAR-PEI
LOOKS YEARS
YOUNGER

ANTI
WRINKLE
CREAM

remarkable resemblance to pets happily installed in British homes like Mrs Block's in 1972. But one of the rarest breeds has to be the Siberian husky. When four of these quickest of sled dogs were born in Switzerland in 1966, experts reckoned there were only fifty of them in the whole of Europe.

April 1980 saw the public debut of Britain's first Australian cattle pups. The six trouble-makers were born in quarantine while their mother was waiting clearance to join show-business dog trainers John and Mary Holmes from Verwood in Dorset. An interesting way to transport seven dogs from Australia for the price of one!

An Egyptian greyhound shows a remarkable likeness to his ancestor.

Six little Aussies looking for trouble.

The famous pianist, Semprini, was so taken

by the spinone hunting dog from Italy that he brought one back to England in 1957 as a gift for one of the trainers at the well-known Oakleigh kennels at Bracknell in Berkshire. The gesture doubled the number of spinones in Britain at the time! Businessmen in Brazil put much time and effort into trying to find an international market for their country's only purebred dog. Yandu, a fine, if somewhat forbidding, specimen of the Fila Brasileiro breed, was pictured towering above the heads of his handlers as he leapt for meat during a training session. Those brave enough to take on his descendants would have to find at least US$2,000 per pup – and a steady nerve.

Yandu, a dog to be obeyed!

Then again, they could always go for the French bulldog instead. Less Churchillian than the British version, though of equally powerful build, this courageous mastiff is said to be capable of fighting wolves and bears – and presumably just about anything else that gets in its way!

The Akita is equally adept at holding bears at bay, but is better known in its country of origin, Japan, as the kind of dog that mothers are said to be happy to leave looking after their children while they go out shopping. Designated a national monument in Japan, it has a reputation there for combining loyalty and affection with formidable abilities as a guard dog. Like the Egyptian greyhound, its image is found in 4,000-year-old tombs, but its ancient owners would turn in their Japanese graves at the down-to-earth eating habits of the few dozen or so that have found their way into the United Kingdom. One pup predictably named 'Kiskas Geisha Girl' was said to be particularly fond of that British speciality, boiled tripe!

That, at any rate, was the endearing description of the Akita that accompanied its arrival in Britain in 1984. But within six

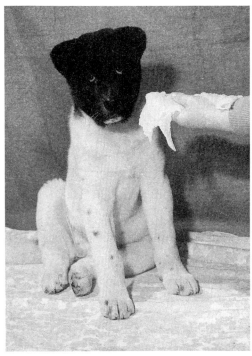

Kiskas Geisha Girl does not seem quite as fond of tripe as was originally reported.

years, the boss of the Battersea Dogs Home was reaching for very different labels. Bill Wadham-Taylor put on display Miko, found straying in South London, and issued a warning that she and her fellow Akitas were taking over from Rottweilers as the fiercest dogs around. 'Everyone,' he warned, 'should be very careful. These are working guard dogs that can be trained to protect. But in the wrong hands they can be very dangerous. The greatest danger is when they fall into the hands of criminals or thugs. Then they can be used to attack and maim people, or for dog fighting. They are certainly not suitable as ordinary pets. 'And,' he went on, 'some people breed them commercially. It can be a profitable business. It seems they are becoming popular, but they're easily capable of killing a baby.' By 1991, Akitas had been embraced by government legislation designed to impose strict controls on the ownership of dangerous dogs. But, apart from the clear differences between the cultures of the two countries, no-one has yet explained satisfactorily why a breed so revered in Japan should be so reviled in Britain.

Perhaps the answer is not to choose any particular breed – however rare it might be – but to go for genuine 'one-offs' – the more endearing mongrels to be found in dogs' homes across the country. Descended from who-knows-where, they are often more loving and lovable. Expert consultant Dr Roger Mugford spoke out boldly before the 1983 Cruft's show. He compiled a list of breeds often seen at the show, but whose temperament, he claimed, was ignored in the extremely competitive race to

'You can't do better than take a mongrel as your pet.'

produce winners. He argued that, outside the competition ring, many beautiful dogs exhibit poor behaviour. His advice? 'You can't do better than take a mongrel as your pet. They may not win prizes, but they're often better balanced'.

Two lovable mongrel pups looking for a home.

THE SMALL, THE TALL
AND THE UGLY

'Like Master, Like Dog' was the title of a Victorian etching, whose creator could be forgiven for a certain artistic licence as

he set about proving the old adage that people actually grow to resemble the dogs they own. A century later, an owner-pet lookalike competition held in Quincy, Massachusetts, provided strong photographic

Spot the owner: Nicholas Chimi and Rip Van Winkle (right) and (below) Sadi and Gina Wildo.

evidence that you don't have to do much growing to look like your pet. Nine-year-old Nicholas Chimi carried off first prize by

proving he was a dead ringer for his St Bernard puppy, Rip Van Winkle. Alas, no prizes for Gina Wildo and her English bull terrier, Sadi, when they entered a similar contest in Houston; but their matching black eyes were a real knockout with the photographers!

One competition in Britain in 1977 saw owners keeping a particularly low profile, just in case people jumped to the wrong conclusions. Its title – 'Scruff of the Year'! But, as far as dogs are concerned, scruffiness is clearly a

Scruffiness is clearly a badge to be worn with pride.

badge to be worn with pride – thousands of pets were sufficiently enamoured of their dishevelled appearance to inundate the *Daily Mirror* newspaper, who organised the competition, with pictures. There was no doubting who should collar the first prize. Step up Rogan, a three-year-old mongrel of rascally parentage, owned by Mrs Dorothy Winup of Bingley in Yorkshire. His tramp-like exterior concealed an intelligence that had already won him several

Rogan – scruffy and proud of it.

prizes in local obedience competitions – making him bright enough to share his mistress's clear pleasure in the £500 reward.

Facing page
Scruffy by name, scruffy by nature.

Ten years later the search for the country's scruffiest dog was on again. Once more, thousands of dowdy entries poured in – and this time the champion ragbag was...

The uglier the dog, the more he or she is loved.

er, Scruffy. This moth-eaten mongrel was the pride and joy of Elizabeth Jones from Pentre in South Wales. She described the secret of his success: 'When he is laying down he is so shaggy you can't tell which end is which. People are amazed when he gets up and they suddenly realise they have been talking to the wrong end'.

Usually, the uglier the dog, the more he or she is loved. One sad exception was Bert the two-year-old mongrel, whom nobody wanted. It mattered not that he was bright and friendly. Would-be owners inspecting the dogs at the RSPCA home at Hatch Beauchamp in Somerset in 1985, were repelled by his appearance – because his lower jaw was too big, and his bottom teeth stuck out permanently – earning him nicknames like 'Goofy', 'Jaws' and 'Dracula'.

The supervisor of the home, Sarah Jones, delicately explained the

Looking for affection, Bert puts on a brave, but somewhat bizarre, face.

problem: 'It's quite unusual to see a dog looking as odd as this, and it does tend to put people off. He was picked up as a stray more than a month ago and no-one has even thought about taking him. All the other dogs here are so much better looking. It's so sad. He's very affectionate and good natured. He'd make a super pet. He really loves everyone – but they don't love him back!'

'He really loves everyone – but they don't love him back.'

No such problems for Rose the bulldog, who went overboard with celebratory kisses when she was pronounced the Ugliest Dog in Yorkshire at a show in Holmfirth in 1979. On the receiving end, her owner, Mrs Thelma Hallawell, obviously not fully used to 'great slobbering wet ones' of that size and

Mrs Hallawell seems to find it difficult to look Rose in the face.

A 'slew-eyed, bent-toothed, bow-legged, would-be Boston Terrier'

persistence. But she didn't mind. 'Rose,' she said, 'is just a great big softie at heart.' That same year, the dog judges hired by the *Boston Sunday Globe* had very little difficulty thinning down almost a hundred entries to home in on the Ugliest Dog in New England. Their undisputed champion was a 'slew-eyed, bent-toothed, bow-legged, would-be Boston Terrier' named Pudge. 'This guy,' said his owner, Vera Mulvehill, 'is as dumb as he looks.'

Left *No difficulty finding adjectives to describe Pudge.* Below *Chi-Chi, the ugliest of them all.*

But perhaps not as dumb as Chi-Chi, a nine-year-old Turkish Naked who padded off with the Ugliest Dog in the World title at Petaluma, California; and not nearly as *offended* as Solo, who hit the headlines in Burgess Hill in Sussex in 1982. She was possibly the only dog to become the victim of a poison pen campaign. 'I think you are the ugliest dog I have ever seen' was the opening gambit in an anonymous, typewritten letter dropped through the letterbox. And Solo's owner, Mrs Joyce Laing, was even more annoyed by the suggestion that followed: 'Why don't you get your master or mistress to take you for a face-

Solo finds consolation in her fan mail.

lift?' The hate mail continued with a second missive, this time with a paper bag enclosed, along with the suggestion that it should be placed over the poor creature's head. Then came the final barb: 'I think the best thing about you is your tail'! The only consolation for Solo was that when the local newspaper picked up the story, they were inundated with letters from fans anxious to counter the ugly claims. Even for dogs, beauty is in the eye of the beholder.

For many years, the USA held the record for the world's heaviest dog – a giant St Bernard that weighed in at a ground-shaking 295 pounds (that's 21st 1lb). It was only the intervention of a vet that prevented a British St Bernard from mounting a serious bid for the title in 1980. Jason, whose home was the Fox and Hounds pub at Billesdon, near Leicester, had to go on a special diet after his owner, Nick Plummer, was advised that his pet was 'dangerously overweight'. So the portly St Bernard could only slobber with envy – and commendable restraint – as Nick's grand-daughter, Rachel, settled down beside him to tuck provocatively into an ice cream.

Seven years earlier, it was another hound called Jason who held the title of (the then) Heaviest Dog in Britain. Although he tipped the scales at a paltry 238 pounds, this five-year-old English Mastiff was still capable of inflicting serious injury just by treading on your foot! Josephine Skinner,

'I think you are the ugliest dog I have ever seen.'

from Worthing in Sussex, bought him when he was a gangling twenty-pound puppy, a mere seven weeks old. She started him 'gently' on a daily diet of 24 raw eggs and a pound of meat – and he just grew and grew! Later, to maintain his adult frame, he happily munched his way through four pounds of meat a day – swelling his ample measurements to a 54in chest, a 46in waist and a 33in neck.

An envious Jason watches his waistline.

But what do you do when a dog that size fancies accompanying its owners on holiday? Tom and Ann Munday found that no hotel or boarding house would take their 252-pound Old English Mastiff, Leo, because of his size. Even

More than she bargained for – Josephine Skinner and the puppy that kept on growing.

25

Breakfast in bed – a holiday treat for Leo.

boarding *kennels* rejected him! So they decided that holidays on wheels were the only answer. For them – a swanky, new motor caravan; for Leo – a ten-foot-long mini caravan which could be towed behind them. 'It was,' insisted Mr Munday, 'the only answer.'

There were no reports on the holiday plans of Zorba the Great, who loped into the *Guinness Book of Records* to take the title of the World's Heaviest Dog in 1988. But it was generally assumed that he was enjoying a life of luxury in London with his master, millionaire property owner Chris Eraclides. A mere 15 pounds when he arrived as a puppy, four hearty meals a day pushed Zorba up to 17 stone by the age of

two. Breakfast snacks consisting of a pint of milk, two egg yolks, honey and cereal wheat biscuits helped take him to a mighty 315 pounds by the time he was six – earning him that place in the record books.

Zorba would barely have noticed Kildonan Chocolate Drop, let alone acknowledge that he belonged to the same species. Kildonan – a prime example of the smallest breed of dog in the world, the Chihuahua, entered life weighing just one ounce. Even when fully grown he barely topped one pound, and was just over half way there when the *Daily Mirror* caught up with him to put his statistics to the test in the summer of 1961. His owner, Mrs Elizabeth Mackie of Glasgow, thought him a delicate puppy, even for a Chihuahua, and strengthened his diet with extra milk which she persuaded him to take from an eye drop dispenser. Kildonan Chocolate Drop made the headlines, but not the record books. According to the *Guinness Book of Records*, the smallest dog in the world was a Yorkshire terrier which grew no heavier than ten ounces, even when fully grown.

Half a pound of Chocolate Drop.

Inevitably, there is also a running competition to produce the tallest dog in the world – with loving humans doing their best to give nature a helping hand. Hamlet the Great Dane wolfed down five pounds of meat a day, topped up with an

Facing page
*Dominic seems
keen to play with
his new friend.*

unlimited supply of dog biscuits, as his owner, Fred Philby of Leigh-on-Sea, Essex, limbered him up for the 1970 champion stakes. The measurement has to be to the shoulders (presumably just to make sure no advantage is given to dogs with unusually tall heads!). By the age of two, Hamlet was able to equal the then British record of 38 inches – and even towered unnervingly above Fred when the two of them shared a settee together. No wonder Fred's other dog, the diminutive Piggy the papillon, of indeterminate parentage, perched on a cushion – just to make sure he was noticed.

Another Great Dane, three-year-old Dominic, made a bid for the title three years later under the guidance of Mrs Iris Bates of Harlow in Essex. He managed 40 inches – to what must have been the deep despair of the kitten dragooned into his company to provide the photographer with a dramatic sense of perspective.

But even Dominic was shown a clean pair of shoulders by Danzas - yet another Great Dane. His 40½ inches earned him the title of Tallest Dog in the World in 1980. Just for the record,

Danzas wants a few more miles but his 'minder' pleads for mercy!

he also weighed a staggering 16 stone and measured 44 inches round his chest. No wonder his owner, Peter Comley of Milton Keynes, had to take him on daily eight-mile walks just to keep his pet fit.

But no dog has his day for too long in the record books – and no breed either. In the mid-Seventies, an Irish wolfhound called Kelly touched 39 inches when just one year old. The Cosser family of Herne Bay in Kent knew they were on to something big, and so, a year later, when Kelly hit 41 inches, they spent several thousand pounds building the hound a special extension to the family home in the shape of a king-size kennel. No-one knew how long Kelly would be around to enjoy it – or whether he would target another canine record – that

His owner had to take him on daily eight-mile walks.

of the *oldest* dog in the world. Ageism certainly seemed in fashion in the pet world in the early 1980s. Innkeeper Fritz Schittenheim, of Benheim in Germany, offered Dackel Jockel when his elderly dachshund turned 21. Although rather deaf, Jockel still had good eyesight and 'yelped well', but all he could manage was the West German title. In Britain, honours went to a mongrel called Rex, who chalked up 23 comfortable years and five months before passing away at the home of his owner, Miss Maria Fox of Ledbury near Hereford. But they were both shown a clean pair of heels by Chilla, a cross between a black Labrador and an Australian cattle dog. Owner David Gordon of the Queensland Gold Coast reported that Chilla died in his sleep at the ripe old age of 32 – the equivalent of 217 human years!

And just in case you think there is a limit to the range of such canine competitions, a two-and-a-half-year-old basset hound called Varlet made his bid for the history books at the 1959 Cruft's Dog show in London. He challenged other bassets to see who had the longest ears. With his measuring 26 inches from tip to tip, Varlet seemed confident of outright victory – to say nothing of a headline or two.

Varlet displays his prize features.

HOOLIGAN HOUNDS

You may have loved a dog through thick and thin, through good times and bad times, but you will never have had to put up with the litany of hooliganism which a ten-stone Newfoundland called Duke inflicted upon his unfortunate Nottinghamshire owners. Stanley and Olive Harding were left almost permanently in the wars by the way he threw his weight around. He seriously injured Stanley twice, knocked Olive out cold, and cut and bruised them both.

Nursing their injuries, Olive and Stanley Harding set off for 'walkies' with Duke.

First Stanley, a 48-year-old engineer, slipped four discs in his back lifting Duke into a bath. Then his shoulder was dislocated when Duke took *him* for a walk. Olive fell victim when Duke tried to be gently playful and knocked her flat. But the Hardings insisted that their dog was still a real, loveable pet. 'Just a bit clumsy' was the way Stanley delicately put it!

John Wilson, from Durham, spent a lot of time teaching his Alsatian to do all kind of tricks - until the dog managed a trick too far. John had trained him to copy him when he locked up his shed each night - which was all jolly useful until the Alsatian slipped the bolt across while John was still on the wrong side. The one thing he hadn't taught the intelligent hound was how to *undo* the bolt. John spent the whole night locked in the shed!

When a fireman succeeds in putting out a fire, you would think his worries were over. Not for Helmut Ruck, called to tackle a blaze in a house in Bonn. He soon dowsed the flames - but couldn't leave the building because a ferocious

The one thing he hadn't taught the intelligent hound was how to undo the bolt.

Great Dane had him pinned against the wall. A neighbour helpfully volunteered the information that 'only one person can make the dog obey him, and that's the son of the house who is staying with his aunt in the town centre'. A fire-engine hastily made the round trip to collect eight-year-old Franz Heymann, whose brisk command soon called the dog to heel.

Another dog got rescuers in a lather when he was spotted marooned on a sandbank off the coast near San Francisco. A power boat rushed out to pick the animal up, but its engine failed just before it got there. The dog then calmly swam to shore - while a lifeboat was launched to rescue the power boat crew.

Heike was a another dog with a lot to answer for. Her habit of picking up the telephone whenever it rang caused an international police alert in March 1983. Heike had lifted up the receiver when Frenchman Michel Corre tried to put a call through from Paris to the dog's owner, Helen Rowbotham, at her home in Scunthorpe. The odd gruffling noises down the phone alarmed him. So he did the most sensible thing and phoned the Humberside police. They, in turn, sent along a team of local bobbies, all poised for action. As they were preparing to break down the door to free Mrs Rowbotham from the ruffians holding her, a neighbour rushed out to explain what might have happened. Normally Mrs Rowbotham - ever mindful of her pet's unusual interest in telecommunications - covered the phone with a cushion when she went out without Heike. This time she forgot.

Heike stops the ringing.

Another dog with the law on his tail was Shackle, an Alsatian-Labrador left alone in the house, who got hold of the push-button handset while it was ringing. Upset by the noise, he began munching the phone like a bone - and somehow caught the '9' button three times in a row. All the emergency operator could hear was growling and barking. Was it someone being attacked by a mad hound? Or a robbery victim, speechless with shock, whose faithful dog was trying to raise the alarm. The line was kept open, police traced the call to a house at Maldon in Essex, and an ambulance crew raced to the scene.

He began munching the phone like a bone.

Everything appeared normal, but, not wanting to take any chances, the police broke in through some French windows, only to find Shackle cowering and whimpering in a corner - he knew he had done wrong. They left an explanatory note on the kitchen table for owner Sara Dines: 'Your dog has managed to dial 999 and we had to break into your house. Sorry about the window!'

In 1981, residents of the Dabbs Hill Lane area of Northolt in Middlesex were told that in future they had to collect their own letters and parcels from the local post office. The reason was a seven-pound terrier called Sammy, who had taken a dislike to

postmen ever since one hit him across the head with a bag. In the words of the Area Head Postmaster, John Butcher: 'This dog is an entirely fearless creature. It has not taken chunks out of my staff, but it has genuinely frightened them'. In all, 83 homes were boycotted until Sammy's owner, Elizabeth Wyatt, promised that Sammy would always be kept locked up at delivery times.

The Chapman family had two Alsatians whose bite was as good as their bark. A judge in England ordered them to be put down after they bit two people. So, to protect their pets, the Chapmans moved house - to South-West France. A clean-sheet start for them - but not for the Alsatians, who promptly attacked the customs officer welcoming them to France.

Marie Davis, of Dagenham in Essex, had to give away her troublesome hound. He was an over-lively Jack Russell. His problem? He kept biting one of her other dogs - an eleven-stone Rottweiler.

Little dogs can be expensive as well as being holy terrors. A giraffe dropped dead in the ring of a Munich circus after being chased by a dachshund. The owners of the big top promptly sued the dog's owner for £35,000 in compensation.

'MAN SHOOTS DOG' - a common enough occurrence in some Mediterranean countries where the hunting season is considered an excuse to shoot anything that moves. But occasionally the roles are reversed. 'DOG SHOOTS MAN' was a headline that surfaced in a Johannesburg newspaper in 1956. Barry Lampbrecht was leaning inside his car to reach a loaded shotgun when his dog trod on the trigger, wounding Mr Lampbrecht in the side. He was lucky. In 1991, the Belgian daily Vers L'Avenir reported an incident in which a dog killed his owner. It happened at Ligny, about 25 miles south-east of Brussels. A French Spaniel jumped onto the back seat of a jeep where his master had left a gun, and set the weapon off as the vehicle was being driven down an unpaved road. 66-year-old Jean Guillaume was struck in the back and died on the spot. The blame properly fell not on his dog, but on the person who left a loaded gun with the safety catch off on the back seat.

His dog trod on the trigger

WORKING DOGS

Talk of working dogs, and you conjure up images of them rounding up sheep, guiding the blind, tracking criminals, or sniffing out drugs and explosives. Those occupations are now routine in the canine world. There is however an elite corps of dogs down through history who have cornered rarer niches in the human workplace. An 1893 issue of the journal *Lightning* recorded its 'great pleasure in introducing readers to Miss Strip, the clever little fox terrier which lays the mains of the Crompton Company'.

Attention had apparently been called to 'this promising young electrician' by a note in the *Daily Graphic*. Further investigations revealed the full complexity and cleverness of Miss Strip's technique, developed during three years' experience in the Kensington and Notting Hill areas of London. 'The culverts in which the mains are laid are constructed with cast-iron girders approximately every hundred yards apart, which she cannot pass. She is therefore put into the culverts through one of the house-service boxes, and first runs, with the line fastened to her collar, one way, until she reaches the cast-iron girders, when the line is detached. She then runs back and takes the other end of the line to the other extreme end of the culvert. The dog cannot get out at the ends of the culverts on account of the cast-iron girders, and has to return each time to the place at which she entered. Every 15 yards she has to jump over or squeeze her way past the supporting insulator bars which are built into the concrete. Messrs Crompton and Co declare that they would have great difficulty in getting their work done without the animal, which is the most useful main-laying tool they possess!'

A beagle called Timmy landed a job as a termite detector for an extermination company in Atlanta, Georgia, who promoted his skills as 'the state of the art as far as termites are concerned'. At the equivalent of £85 a call, Timmy would unerringly sniff out any of the tiny creatures daring to munch their way through your property. So reliable was he that an insurance company was prepared to guarantee his accuracy up to a limit of $500,000 – possibly the first time that the renowned sensitivity of a dog's nose had been underwritten by an insurance company.

The first time that the renowned sensitivity of a dog's nose had been underwritten by an insurance company.

In 1957, the Gare du Nord railway station in Paris employed three dogs, Coquette, Rita and Zonzon, for the sole purpose of catching rats. They became great favourites with the travellers – not least because of the unusual way they collected their 'wages', in the shape of titbits saved up for them by the chefs on the dining cars. Over the years, the clever rat-catchers got to know the timetable of every train with a dining car, and made sure they were always there to meet them.

There were no obvious rewards for mongrel terrier Kim. He simply loved the man-sized job he appointed himself to in 1969 at West Loch Tarbert pier in Scotland. As a key dockyard worker, he played a vital role in mooring the 577-ton, 190-foot-long ferry 'Lochiel' when she arrived at the jetty

Kim waits for his boat to come in.

every morning. A reporter described his technique thus: 'As the Lochiel steams into view, Kim is waiting on the quayside. His head is still. His eyes hold concentration worthy of the captain himself. As the first rope snakes out from the ship's bow, Kim darts to where he knows it will land. He grabs it. Then the dockers take over to secure the line. The Lochiel swings through 180 degrees and a second rope is thrown from the stern. Kim splashes into the loch to fetch it. He pulls. The dockers pull. And, clinging by his teeth, Kim gets a lift back onto the pier, where, the job completed, he proudly barks a welcome to the ship'.

A huge, hairy cuddle complete with a warm, slurpy kiss and an affectionate rub from her cold, wet nose.

A lovable St Bernard named Sherry produced the animal world's answer to all those kissograms delivered by scantily clad girls. She went into business in 1984 with the 'nuzzlegram' – a huge, hairy cuddle complete with a warm, slurpy kiss and an affectionate rub from her cold, wet nose. Sherry's owner, Sarah Newbury, who operated this big, friendly service in the Wiltshire town of Trowbridge, described it as 'an unforgettable experience'. She reassured doubtful potential customers: 'There's no need to be put off by Sherry's size. When she puts her arms around you, it's just a gentle clasp...sheer bliss!'

Pub owner George Howe employed a three-stone boxer dog called Tulsa to carry his takings to the bank. He reckoned the three-year-old stray

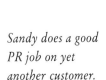

he saved from being put down was more than a match for any cosh bandits or muggers. So, once a week, three-year-old Tulsa was entrusted with a briefcase containing hundreds of pounds, which he gripped firmly in his teeth and delivered safely to the bank 200 yards down the road. In fact, standing on two legs, he even lifted the heavy bag onto the counter. George, a former Foreign Office official who ran the Tarleton Arms at Southport in 1966, testified: 'We soon found he had a passion for carrying things. I only have to say "bank", and he sets out on his own. He's better than any security guard. Heaven help the thief who tries to take the money'.

Little Sandy was a cairn terrier with what you might describe as a jewel of a job, mixing with the rich, the beautiful and the famous. In 1978, he appeared on the payroll of international jewellers, Mappin and Webb, as a 'customer relations officer' – at £2 a week, plus as many of his favourite chocolates as customers chose to feed him. Sandy's unusual working life had a tragic start. His master Jim Sutherland's wife died, and Jim

Sandy does a good PR job on yet another customer.

thought he'd have to give the dog up. But his bosses at the Mappin and Webb Glasgow shop suggested he bring Sandy into work with him. When some of the firm's rich and influential customers said how much they liked Sandy, the terrier was promptly hired, and, according to manager, Tony Jennings, 'earned his keep over and over again. Women customers just love him, and in his

Brum answers an emergency call.

Right Cresta shows the way.

own way he helps to sell. If he's not about they ask for him'. Added Jim: 'I think the women like him because he helps them to relax when they are looking for something to buy'.

Brum was a two-year-old Alsatian who earned her keep by becoming a mechanic's mate. Owned by a Mr Randall of Wanstead in Essex, the dog displayed a most helpful talent that took him into the headlines in 1937. Not content with carrying out his guard duties at his master's garage, or regularly waiting to collect the letters from the postman, Brum would also hand out tools to the mechanics when they wanted them. If one of the men called out "hammer", the Alsatian would dutifully trot off to the tool box and bring him one.

Guide dogs for the blind are possibly the hardest working canines around, but the time often comes when they need a bit of help themselves. Labrador Blackie had been the eyes of blind telephonist Jim O'Brien for eleven years, when the dog herself started to go blind. Jim needed a new guide dog, of course, and in 1973 another Labrador, Cresta, arrived to take over. But Jim couldn't face parting with Blackie – so Cresta took on the job of looking after both of them. As the trio walked the streets of Market Harborough, Blackie could proudly boast he

He was the only guide dog with his own guide dog!

was the only guide dog with his own guide dog!

What happens to a working sheepdog when she goes blind? Tib the collie and her owner, farmer Iain Ross, decided it was business as usual – that good ears and canny instinct could make up for the loss of vision. In 1962, sceptics were treated to a demonstration on Over Glinns Farm at Fintry in Stirlingshire. It took just two minutes for seven-year-old Tib, working to shouts and piercing whistles, to round up 100 sheep spread out across a giant field – and another three minutes to pen them. A proud Mr Ross paid tribute: 'There are not many sheep dogs that could do that as easily – even with full sight. Tib's blindness was caused by diseased eye nerve-cords. It was impossible to save her sight, but I never had any thoughts of having her destroyed. She'd been well trained, and slowly and patiently we worked together in the fields. Tib has super-sensitive hearing. She can hear my whistles and commands half a mile away.

Tibs has no trouble finding a comfortable seat at the end of a hard day's work.

She knows every inch of my house, and every gate and hedge in the fields. She is a dog in a million. I tried the best vets in the country to try to save her sight, and I would still spend any amount of money if I thought there was a chance. But even so, my wife and I believe Tib is happy, and that we have the most wonderful dog in the world'.

The sheepdog with possibly the least work in the world was Roy, who took full advantage of Gareth Evans's enthusiasm to motorise sheep-farming. Only rarely did Roy get his paws dirty. Most of the time he just kept a watchful eye on things from his lofty perch on the petrol tank of Gareth's motorbike, as they rounded up the flock on their 400-acre farm at Foel Cathan in North Wales. The technique saved them both some weary legwork.

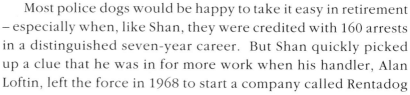

All quiet on the waterfront under Shan's watchful eye.

Most police dogs would be happy to take it easy in retirement – especially when, like Shan, they were credited with 160 arrests in a distinguished seven-year career. But Shan quickly picked up a clue that he was in for more work when his handler, Alan Loftin, left the force in 1968 to start a company called Rentadog

Security Ltd. One of the dog's first, and most unusual, contracts was for Harlow Development Corporation, who called him in after a spate of vicious attacks on ducks and swans on a local pond. As Shan mounted what may well have been the first official canine 'swan-guard', one of Alan's partners confided that it was hardly the toughest of assignments for a dog that had tracked down the infamous triple police killer, Harry Roberts. He was 'confident there would be early developments'.

Army guard dog, Brice, looked on enviously at the strong boots issued to soldiers for square-bashing and long marches. Unusually for an Alsatian, he suffered from sore paws because

Brice, back on the parade ground in his new boots.

the pads of skin on them were too thin. He could just about handle the discomfort at home in England, but, when, in 1983, he was posted to chilly West Berlin with the 3rd Royal Regiment

of Fusiliers, he got cold feet. Instead of growling at the East German border guards, Brice could only manage a whimper – until someone suggested making him a pair of boots! A quick whip-round amongst the troops produced 100 marks for a German cobbler to devise and make the boots. Brice no longer had any excuses to skip guard duty.

Neither, for that matter had Shaun, an Irish Wolfhound adopted as the Irish Guards' mascot in 1960. Part of his early training – before he was allowed to march in front of the band – was to stand guard over a neat row of bearskins, *Tea-time duty for Shaun.*

temporarily abandoned when his masters marched into Windsor's Victoria barracks for their tea-break.

In 1965, scientists at the Royal Aircraft Establishment at Farnborough tried kitting out Alsatians with two-way radios to see if they would be of any help in search missions. The dogs had sets strapped to their bodies, so they could be given instructions from a distance. The hope was that they would be able to comb inaccessible areas out of voice-range of their handlers, when, for example, looking for fragments of crashed aircraft or survivors. Three-year-old Rusty, one of the Ministry of Aviation's star pupils, turned up at a demonstration at Farnborough to show how he could find a railway ticket in a field while following instructions. But the idea never quite caught on.

Rusty, the radio-controlled Alsatian.

Probably the most dangerous job any dog can be trained to do is search for explosives, ammunition and guns. In 1974, 100 novice Alsatians and Labradors were among the first to be brought to the Royal Army Veterinary Corp's training centre in Leicestershire to learn their craft in a village created specially for them. To make sure

A Veterinary Corps recruit checks out a phone box – or perhaps he is on the phone to a girlfriend!

it accurately simulated working conditions in Northern Ireland, the village included nine fully furnished houses, each with removable panels and floorboards, and other hiding places. Also there to be searched were phone boxes, cars, a bus, a train – and even a plane. The village barn was occupied by sheep and goat to get the dogs used to ignoring farmyard smells. The dogs, bought from the public full grown, usually 'graduate' in three months. When trained they can search a house in 20 minutes – something that would take a soldier hours. Their C.O., Colonel Harry Bishop, was not always popular with his canine recruits. He had a golden rule that none of the dogs were allowed to be female. In the battle against terrorists, nothing was allowed to interfere with a chap's concentration!

That kind of painstaking training pays off in other fields too. In 1980, Brumby, a black Labrador, helped Customs and Excise men to uncover one and a half tons of cannabis worth £2 million and heroin valued at £700,000. Some of it was uncovered in suitcase bottoms at Heathrow and in a consignment of antiseptic cream sent from Nepal. The drug coups earned Brumby the title 'Sniffer of the Year' – top dog in the pack of 18 Labradors meticulously trained by the RAF to hunt down drugs in airports,

He had a golden rule that none of the dogs were allowed to be female.

docks and post office sorting counters.

Possibly the first scout dog to be flown by helicopter to join a military patrol was York, an Alsatian called in to help American troops guarding the truce line in Korea in 1954. Travelling in a home-made cage strapped to the side of the helicopter, he was ferried regularly to the part of the line where he was needed most. Newspapers at the time explained that York 'is invaluable on patrol, for his sharp ears soon detect any unusual noises or movements, and his quiet attack gives no warning to communists attempting to infiltrate across the line'.

Topping that with ease in 1962 was Tudor, a five-year-old

York on his way to the front line.

Tudor launches himself during training at Aldershot.

golden Labrador being trained by the 23rd Parachute Field Ambulance Brigade to make a parachute drop to help in mountain rescue work. His first jump from an aircraft was scheduled to take place over Aldershot. Presumably he remembered to bend his knees on landing!

Few stories illustrate the resilience, dedication and tenacity of the highly-trained dog better than that of Major, an Alsatian who set off after a robber trying to escape from a police ambush near Cardiff in 1983. In his desperation, the thief climbed up a 120-foot quarry face, crashed through dense woodland and then swam a river. But despite all that he couldn't shake off the police dog. The *Weekly News* reported that when Major failed to respond to his handler's call, it was thought he had drowned in the river, and the search for him was called off. 'Four hours later, an inspector spotted the bedraggled dog sitting on a doorstep. But when he went over to take it home, Major refused to budge. The house was

An inspector spotted the bedraggled dog sitting on a doorstep.

searched and found to be empty. Still the dog refused to move. Finally he was allowed into the house to search, and found the robber hiding in a wardrobe. In court, the man was jailed for six months after admitting burglary charges.'

Inexplicably, the 1970s saw a spate of ladder-climbing dogs exciting the interest of the tabloids. Nicholas Murray, who ran the Wellington Hotel in London's Shepherd's Bush was climbing a 60-foot ladder to carry out some repairs to the roof when he looked round and found his 15-month-old Jack Russell terrier, Bobby, right behind him. Ladders were equally irresistible to Chester, a somewhat heavier six-year-old Labrador retriever who accompanied builder, Dave Coogan, on his roofing work around Mountain Lakes, New Jersey. And to Bo, another steeple-Jack Russell who carefully supervised the roof repair work undertaken by Eric Spencer at Deddington in Oxfordshire. For five years, whenever Eric and his son John climbed onto a roof, Bo followed them up the rungs – no matter how great the height. His only problem was that he never mastered the art of getting down on his own.

His only problem was that he never mastered the art of getting down on his own.

Ben, an adventurous two-year-old Staffordshire bull terrier cross, fancied the job of window-cleaner's mate right from the word go. Out on the rounds for the first time around the Lancashire towns of Burnley and Nelson in 1979, he shinned up the ladder before his master, Paul Duxbury, could wring out his chamois leather. And even if he couldn't lend a paw in the proper sense of the phrase, Ben was at least great company – as well as a lively conversation piece for puzzled passers-by.

A lively conversation piece for puzzled passers-by.

A six-year-old mongrel, Sandy, also caught the bug,

Sandy, a shaggy face at the upstairs window.

accompanying Steve Hulbert up his 30-foot ladder as he brightened the windows of Ashton-under-Lyne in 1984. 'She's got a good head for heights', said Steve, 'and is so well known that she's just been made an honorary member of the Manchester Sky Divers' Club.' Which might just imply that this was one dog that *had* found a way of returning to terra firma on her own!

But for serious – as opposed to pretend – work, you would have to go a long way to beat the huskies whose muscle-power drives the transport in snow-bound territories of the world. At one time, those visitors who disembarked at the Eigergletscher railway station, just below the awesome sea of ice that forms the Jungfrau glacier, were greeted by 27 Greenland dogs. Renowned and willing fighters as far as other dogs were concerned, with people they were harmless, trustful and faithful to a high degree. So it was no surprise that they were entrusted with the task of drawing the sledges that carried the tourists out across the frozen waste. Happiest when the weather was at its worst, they were originally brought to the

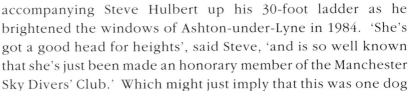

Jungfrau to keep railway employees at the top in touch with the valley below whenever severe winter storms closed the line.

Bothie, a fluffy, curly-haired mongrel, landed the job of mascot for the Transglobe Expedition, an historic journey that took in both the North and South poles, and lasted from 1979 to 1982. Stubborn and stone deaf whenever he chose to be, Bothie resolutely refused to be house (or even tent) trained. But during the long months of travel, often in extreme circumstances, he became an entertainer who never let his audience down. So much so that his owners, explorers Ranulph and Virginia Fiennes wrote a book – Bothie the Polar Dog – as a tribute to his resilience and good humour.

Bothie, an explorer with a mind of his own.

And perhaps the most frustrating and thankless task ever inflicted on a dog was that which befell three beagle hounds, specially flown from America to Nepal in 1958 to join a Himalayan expedition hunting for the 'mysterious, giant, hairy, human-like creature' known as the abominable snowman. It was the first time in the century-old history of Himalayan mountaineering that dogs had been allowed to accompany such an expedition. Special permission had to be obtained from the Nepal government for the three hounds to visit the 'holy' heights of the Himalayas, as dogs are regarded by that country as 'unholy' animals. Nothing was found – the abominable snowman lived to hype another day.

He became an entertainer who never let his audience down.

Some dogs will try absolutely anything to keep themselves in work!

STUDS AND RESULTS

Bruce, an award-winning Old English bulldog, had a good excuse for looking permanently dog-tired. Back in November 1978, he celebrated becoming a daddy for the 400th

The bulldog breed as personified by Bruce (above) and Tim (below right).

Known to his admirers as Tantalising Tim.

time. And for the last two, he never even met the mother. Four-year-old Bruce stayed at home in Aldridge in the West Midlands. The mother, Katie, was in Holland, and the birth was achieved by artificial insemination. Such was the worldwide clamour for British bulldogs; and it was still going strong seven years later, when scores of lady bulldogs were clamouring for the £500-a-time services of Annadic Riptide, known to his admirers as Tantalising Tim. The bulldog spirit of this superstud was required at least five or six times a week. His owner, Sally Griffiths-Plummeridge from Bilsington in Kent, admitted that it was heavy going, but she added: 'He's only 18 months old and could carry on until he's eight, fathering up to 1,000 pups along the way'. No wonder his tongue was hanging out!

Robin the bashful Peke found that the

ladies left him cold. Attractive young brides-to-be vied all day for the affections of this 18-month-old romeo. But he ignored them all from the moment he arrived at the stud in the Berkshire village of Hampstead Marshall in 1967. Even leaving Robin with as many as six girl Pekes at a time failed to move him. He sometimes insulted them unforgivably by dozing off just as they were making up to him. Pekingese breeder, Lisa Gray, gave the potential champion an ultimatum – choose a bride within three days or be banished to life as a mere family pet. When the story hit the national newspapers, Robin was inundated with offers from would-be owners. This time they were of a kind that he just couldn't refuse.

Hamlet the basset hound had no such troubles. He'd sired 1,793 puppies, and was showing no signs of flagging, when an unfortunate accident brought his amorous career to a sudden halt. The tragedy happened in 1972 when his owner, Keith Keen, from Kilburn in North London, took Hamlet to the park for a run. The hound was given two small rubber balls to play with and, when the time came to go home, he turned up with just one of them. Mr Keen just assumed the other had been lost – until poor Hamlet went a bit off colour. An X-ray revealed that he'd swallowed the missing ball, which had lodged in his groin. The operation that followed seemed successful – until Hamlet was put to stud with seven bitches, and

Unmoved, Robin turns his back on more would-be brides.

51

Hamlet bemoans the end of a busy career, in direct contrast to poor Pepe (below right).

each time refused to deliver the goods.

Pepe the pedigree puppy was never the success in the mating game that his owner Susan Liddle intended. The problem was that the poor little chap didn't have any credentials. It was only when she took him to the vet in Salford for a booster injection that Pepe's vital parts were found to be missing. 'He's neither use nor ornament' was how Susan put it, far from pleased that she'd forked out £65 to buy him from a breeder. But her children, Samantha and Joanna, came to the rescue, proving that there was one kind of affection that Pepe would never lack.

Tiny the poodle was another dog who didn't measure up to being a stud. Every time he tried to mate he failed by inches; for nine-inch-high Tiny simply wasn't tall enough to reach the lady toy poodles who towered above him at an elegant 15 inches. His owner, Jackie Brewer of Witham in Essex, tried standing him on telephone books, but even that didn't help. 'The poor thing tried so hard,' she said, 'but all attempts at mating him ended up with both dogs panting around the kitchen. When last reported on, in 1985, Mrs Brewer had thoughtfully bought a poodle crossed with a Yorkshire terrier.

The poor little chap didn't have any credentials.

Tiny's days of frustration were over!

Tiny's days of frustration were over!

Ben the Jack Russell left a tell-tale trademark when he roamed the streets of Manchester indulging in one labour of love after another. His pups - like their dad - were all tail-less. Owner, Graham Ward, was forced to end his pet's gallivanting days and put him on a lead, when no fewer than 20 angry owners identified Ben as the father of their pups.

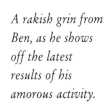

The shock was rather more severe for the owner of Della, a pedigree Alsatian who was duly mated with another fine example of her kind. But love will find a way through any arranged marriage, and it became clear when the ten pups were born that Della had another love in her life, for four of them were nearer to Labrador than Alsatian. The mystery was cleared up for owner Mary Watson, of Woking in Surrey, when the vet explained that a bitch can mate twice, and have puppies of both breeds.

A rakish grin from Ben, as he shows off the latest results of his amorous activity.

So much for the vagaries of fathers! Canine *motherhood* manifests itself in equally diverse ways. Rikki, a 20-month-old Corgi, refused to leave her four pups when fire broke out in the shed where they lived at Warborough in Oxfordshire. She stayed with them even when called by her owner, Dorothy Richards,

Rikki with two of the pups she saved.

Facing page Mealtime for Dixie's foster family.

Sally, back in charge of her pups.

moving them around the shed to try to escape the flames. Rikki was eventually found badly scorched, lying protectively over three of her pups. The fourth had died. The brave Corgi was later give a National Pets Club medal for bravery.

In 1961, a valuable pregnant Airedale, Jean, bolted from Carlisle railway station while being transported from Kilmarnock to the Midlands. Nine weeks later she was found in a rabbit hole – with 11 two-day-old pups.

Bulldog Dixie, who sadly lost all eight of her puppies at birth, became the proud foster-mother of six bulldog pups whose mother had died giving birth. Dixie's owner, Betty Cassidy of Rossendale in Lancashire, said 'it's a chance in a million that both bulldogs gave birth at the same time'.

Retired farmer Ralph Heslop had no hesitation in taking over when his dachshund, Sally, gave birth to an unusually large litter of eight puppies – and was so weak she couldn't feed them. Unwilling to drown them, Mr Heslop sat in front of his living-room fire hand-feeding them every two hours with a teaspoon. He kept it up for 40 cold winter days and nights before neighbours in the village of Wetherall in Cumberland persuaded him to show the results to the world.

Duke, by contrast, couldn't wait to display his four new daughters and three sons. But then the Old English sheepdog was the TV star of a series of famous paint advertisements. So popping the four-week-old puppies into 2.5 litre cans seemed a perfectly natural thing

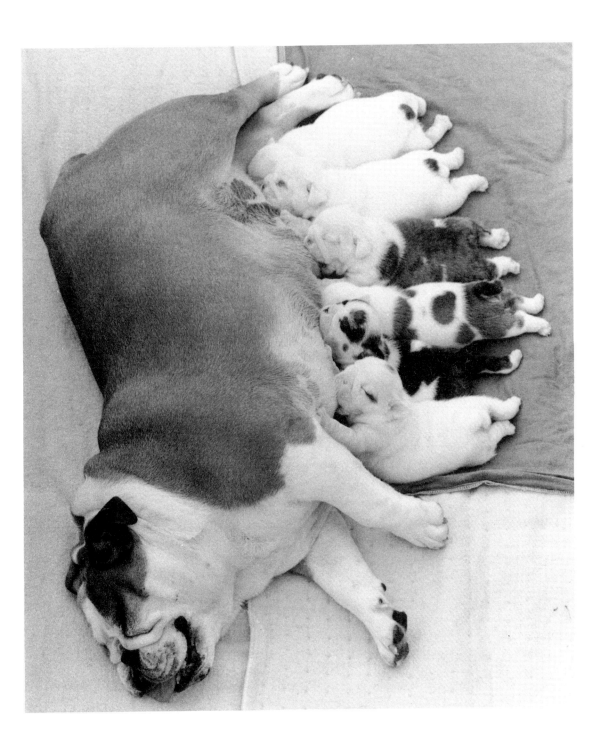

to do – at least for the photographer. Jolly useful too, for catching those little accidents!

In 1955, Mr Bickford of Chingford in Essex claimed a world record for a litter of 14 boxer puppies, whelped by the 20-month old Demon Queen. She fed them in two batches of seven – and hopefully was able to recognise those from the first sitting who tried coming round again for seconds. A year later, Vera Telfer's boxer, Lady Pixie, matched that, but needed a little help at feeding time when her 'stand and deliver' technique wasn't quite enough. Vera had to supply meal supplements in 14 separate bowls – at every single feeding-time.

Promotional photocall for Duke and his family.

Demon Queen's world-record line-up.

Her 'stand and deliver' technique wasn't quite enough.

In 1971, Mollie's Thrill, a Great Dane who had been one of a litter of 13 photographed for the *Daily Mirror*, decided to go one better by producing 14 pups herself. Needless to say, they made it into the paper too - even if one of them decided not to put on her best face for the camera!

Above *Mollie's Thrill tries to keep her pups in line for their photograph.*
Left *Lady Pixie does her best to satisfy her eager youngsters.*

Five years earlier, 15 St Bernard pups managed to flop onto one garden seat for their first public appearance. Just 20 days old, they stayed under the watchful eye of their father, Tello V. Sauliant, and their mother, Snowranger Agamemnon. Owner Clare Bradley, of Mill Farm Kennels near Aylesbury, had a thing about Greek mythology, and borrowed heavily from it to name the pups as they popped out. 'First there was Leander; next were Lysander, Laertes, Leonidas, and Laomedon; then came Lucretia, Lorinda, Laodomia, Letitia, Leonora; followed by Lisette, Lucinda,

Agamemnon's classical litter.

Lorelei, Lampetia; and lastly, Lyric.

Clearly, feeding is the problem – in the early days at least. Sabra the Great Dane had 18 pups in all, but two of them died at birth. To give her a helping hand with the rest, owner Rachel English filled up baby bottles with milk and scattered them around Sabra's sleeping quarters. The Californian newspaper that reported the birth came up with a neat way of explaining that there was no alternative:

'16 mouths to feed – and only ten places at the dinner table.'

'What's a mother to do when she has 16 mouths to feed – and only ten places at the dinner table?'

Dogs welcome all the human help they can get in giving their offspring a good start in life. But sometimes that help can make all the difference in ensuring that they have any offspring at all. Through all the tales of cruelty – of unwanted puppies being bundled into sacks and cardboard boxes and thrown into lakes and rivers – few end as remarkably and happily as a story which aroused a wave of indignation in national newspapers in the winter of 1955:

'A passerby found Kim by the side of a road just outside Farnborough – a little black poodle, crouched motionless in the grass. She didn't move when he called to her. She *couldn't* move; she was literally solid with ice – frozen to the ground.

A few extra places at Sabra's dinner table.

'He picked up the pathetic, unwanted little body and carried it to the light and warmth of a nearby police station. They bathed her in warm water, but she did not stir. It was hard to tell if she were alive or dead. But then they cut the matted fur

Happy ending for Kim the survivor.

around her eyes. They saw life in them – and fear too. She quivered and cowered away from their kind hands. But she drank the warm milk they put in front of her; and she began to get better. A few days later she gave birth to a litter of fine healthy puppies'.

STAR **PAWS**

'Never, *never*, appear with animals or children' is arguably the single most important message that one generation of actors can bequeath to the next. It is a lesson reinforced across the years by theatre reviews from those occasions when the advice was ignored. The human performances become incidental as the critics home in on the animal. A play staged at Astley's Amphitheatre in London in 1846 gave an indication of what the actors were up against in its very title: 'The Dog of the Pyrenees'. Sure enough, the Newfoundland dog filling the title role was duly raved about as 'a splendid, black animal, one of the best of its class'. And, in a paean of praise any actor or actress would kill for, the reviewer goes on: 'Looking at the acting of the hero, one cannot help thinking, from his sagacious head, and the natural, business-like manner in which he sets about everything, that he is actuated by something more than the results of mere training. One of the characters, a mountaineer of the Pyrenees (and that's as close as *he* gets to a mention!), is in prison, tied hands and feet to the wall by cords attached to rings. Emile, who is his companion, is also tied up at some distance. The mountaineer points out a key to the dog, which has been dropped by the gaoler. The dog

Emile, the dog who stole the show.

struggles until he is enabled to slip his head through the collar; and he then undoes the bonds that confine his master, ultimately effecting his deliverance. His sagacity is constantly shown throughout the piece; indeed, as we have stated, the principle interest is centred in Emile; and his performance is one that we recommend to our play-going readers'.

Hardly surprising, then, that dog owners have leapt at the chance to turn their pets into stars of the stage or screen. The producers of the American comedy 'Separate Rooms', which opened at London's Strand Theatre in August 1947, were unable to find the Chihuahua which the plot required. So they advertised in a morning paper for 'The Smallest Dog in London'. Four tiny aspirants duly arrived at the stage door, and if *they* weren't exactly panting with ambition, their owners certainly were!

'He then undoes the bonds that confine his master, ultimately effecting his deliverance.'

Queuing for an audition at the Strand Theatre.

Psyche, who answered the call for 'mongrels only'.

Nine years later, the call went out from the Piccadilly theatre for 'mongrels only' to audition for the part of Plantagenet in a new comedy 'Commemoration Ball', starring Isabel Jeans, Michael Shepley and Norman Wooland. Amongst the hopefuls duly paraded before the cast were Skippy from Maida Vale, Meg from Slough, Peanut from Knightsbridge, Oscar from Bow and Buster from Westminster. But by far the cuddliest creature in the line-up was Psyche, a cross between a collie and a corgi, more than happy to abandon temporarily his Battersea home, and his proud owner, 11-year-old Michael White.

The Royal Shakespeare Company offered what you might call a 'lead role' to a Labrador called Blackie, when it was staging 'Two Gentlemen of Verona' at the Aldwych Theatre in 1970. Playing the part of Crab, he had two big scenes where he was led on stage by the clownish servant, Launce, played by Patrick Stewart. Patrick got Blackie from the Avon Dog Rescue Service, who'd saved him from a destruction centre after he'd been picked up as a stray. From the sidewalk to the footlights in just a few weeks was a discovery story in the finest theatrical tradition.

A discovery story in the finest theatrical tradition.

Another dog that pulled stardom out of the jaws of death was Bomber the Boxer. The lovable all-white dog

'Dirty, flea-ridden and smeared with realistic sores.'

was rejected by breeders because his markings meant he could not be shown as a pedigree. The owner wanted him put down, but a vet's nurse tipped off cement worker, Tony Chapell and his wife Elaine, who came to the rescue. Bomber celebrated his first birthday by landing a part in the 1985 BBCTV production of Charles Dickens's 'Oliver Twist'. His immaculate coat was made up to look 'dirty, flea-ridden and smeared with realistic sores'. But as compensation, he got his own dressing room – and thumbs up for a great performance from the BBC.

Heading in an opposite direction was Shaggy Baggins, star of the hit West End musical '42nd Street', who was sacked after nearly 200 performances alongside the singer Frankie Vaughan. Baggins had to go after the show's director changed a dance routine, and decreed that, instead of making an entrance under his own 'paw-power', the dog would instead have to be carried on stage. Sadly, the nine-year-old Old English sheepdog/border collie crossbreed was just too big and heavy. Baggins' owner, theatrical agent Anne Bishop, threatened to sue the producers of the money-spinning show on the grounds of wrongful dismissal – and asked the actors' union,

Bomber, star of Oliver Twist, at home with his own little 'artful dodger'.

Equity, for help. But a union spokesman said: 'Equity membership is not open to animals – we cannot take up the case!'

A canine replacement called in by a BBC nature film unit got

'Equity membership is not open to animals.'

rather more than she bargained for. Eight hours after arriving on location, a collie called Cathy found she'd been transformed into a fox – with the help of a pair of scissors! Cathy was the

Above *Resting – Baggins looks for work.*
Above right *Cathy is at least in work, but not too happy with her role.*

stand-in for a fox named Basil, who had the starring role in a 1983 documentary about the life of a fox over four seasons. For obvious reasons, Basil couldn't be used when real hounds were around. So the plan was for the newly shorn Cathy to do the long-distance shots, while Basil would save himself for the close-ups. It didn't fool the hounds, but it did fool the cameras.

A collie called Cathy found she'd been transformed into a fox.

The one television programme that has made more dogs famous in Britain than any other is unquestionably the BBC's

'Blue Peter'. To list them here would fill the book, so let it suffice to pay tribute to Honey, the first of several guide dogs for the blind that were trained through the generosity of the programme's legion of young viewers. But other dogs have made their mark on both the small and silver screens in different ways. Kate, 'the Joan Collins of Yorkshire terriers', as her publicity blurb put it, was such a super bitch that she landed a role in Granada TV's soap opera Albion Market. Viewers didn't have much chance to get acquainted – the series was taken off when it failed to make its mark in the ratings.

Above *Soap star Kate and 'friend'.* Below *Bionic screen partners, Lindsay and Maximillian.*

Maximillian, the bionic dog, became established in a more long-running role, partnering Lindsay Wagner in 'The Bionic Woman' TV series, where he had to outrun motorcycles, chew up rifle barrels, bend iron bars and push trucks and vans – with the help of a little trickery, of course. His real name was Alsatian Bracken; and the show's real secret was that he had three stand-ins. Owner Moe Di Sesso confessed 'the job was too difficult for one dog, and as they all look alike... !'

Zero, a two-and-half-year-old mongrel in the early days of the movies, wouldn't have stood for that! The Los Angeles press dubbed him Hollywood's 'wonder dog', or – equally modestly – 'America's foremost canine film performer'. Zero began his training almost the day he was born, and was reputed to be able to perform more tricks for the camera than any dog alive.

Then there was Sir George, a typical British bulldog roped in to star in a Navy film comedy 'The Bulldog Breed'. All the nice girls love a sailor – which is how Sir George became attached to the shapely ankle of production secretary Jean Stoddart!

Furio Caligola used to go walkies with actor Marcello Mastroianni when the two were on location in Milan in 1964, shooting the Marco Ferreri film 'The Man of the Five Balloons'. The two-stone mastiff's 'placid and sophisticated air' made him much in demand with film makers – which explains why Furio was given the red carpet treatment. No mere dog kennel for him! Instead the producers paid for him to have his own room at Milan's Residence Hotel, where a steady stream of 'tasty

Film stars: the drooling Sir George (above) and the rather more dignified Furio (right).

A steady stream of 'tasty and sumptuous meals' helped him maintain his weight.

and sumptuous meals' helped him maintain his weight.

Prince the singer took Britain by storm when he appeared on the TV show 'That's Life' in 1979. Only *this* Prince was a dog. His owner, Paul Allen from Leeds, called him 'a kind of canine crooner' who, on cue, sang words such as cha-cha-cha, scissors and sausages. Predictably, 'Sausages' was the title of his first pop disc, which he produced in a four-hour session at a Manchester recording studio.

'Sausages' was the title of his first pop disc.

Mrs Dorothy Steves of Wraysbury in Buckinghamshire didn't mind her dog doing 'odd jobs' about the house. Radar the Alsatian was not only a good guard dog, but would drag the laundry to the washing machine in the kitchen, take the phone off the hook when it rang, trot off happily to post a letter in the local pillar box, and fetch milk from the doorstep, remembering, of course, to close the door behind him. Wider praise came his way – from millions of TV viewers – for his portrayal of a police dog in the BBC crime series 'Softly, Softly'. When Radar died, he was taken to his last resting place in a mahogany casket, borne by a group of pallbearers. Mrs Steves, carrying a photo of her beloved pet along with his lead and a bone, headed a group of thirty mourners, among them the stars of the series, Frank Windsor and Terence Rigby.

In the case of another successful

Radar, star performer around the house as well as on the screen.

film and TV series, 'Lassie', the producers didn't exactly shout it from the rooftops when the collie that filled the title role went off to the great kennel in the sky. The first cinema blockbuster 'Lassie Come Home' in 1951 was followed by six more films and a top television series, which went on – and on – way beyond the lifespan of any Shetland collie. When Hollywood began work on a new movie 'Lassie, My Lassie' 26 years later, dog trainer Rudd Weatherwax let the dog out of the bag and confirmed what had been long

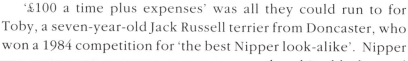

'Boy Shetland collies seem better looking.'

suspected. There had been, in fact, several Lassies. And he also let slip another secret – all of them have been male dogs, because, as he provocatively put it: 'Boy Shetland collies seem better looking'. And there was one other change he had to report – the original collie (whose real name was Pal) earned £100 a week; his successor in the 1975 film was paid a total of £75,000!

'£100 a time plus expenses' was all they could run to for Toby, a seven-year-old Jack Russell terrier from Doncaster, who won a 1984 competition for 'the best Nipper look-alike'. Nipper

Toby recreates a famous image.

was the white, black-eared terrier immortalised as a trade-mark by the record giant HMV as he perched attentively beside an old-fashioned gramophone. Nipper No1 loved nothing better than stealing pheasants and fighting. Nipper No 2 was an expert at 'begging for minutes on end' as he toured the country, posing with stars such as Sting, Margot Fonteyn, Bill Wyman and Boy George to help celebrate HMV's 100th anniversary.

For their 50th anniversary, the dog food manufacturers Spillers brought together K9, the robot dog from BBC Television's 'Dr Who', and Robert, a golden retriever whose lovable face sells half a million packets of their products each week. Generating that kind of buying power, it is hardly surprising that the super-dogs of the TV advertisements are among the most pampered in history. You won't often catch them burying bones – it might make their shampooed, manicured paws dirty! You could tell that just by looking at Henry, the magnificent, true-blue bloodhound

It might make their shampooed, manicured paws dirty!

who, through the Seventies, extolled the delights of Chunky canned dog food and Minced Morsels, along with his look-alike owner, the Liberal MP Clement Freud. But Henry only acquired his TV name when the advertising men got to work on his image. His real name – when at home in his Hampstead pad –

was Sanguine Saturn; and he was a she! To Henry, then, a corner of TV stardom in the Seventies. But the hound that has really dominated TV advertising across three decades – since virtually the start of commercial television in Britain – has been the Dulux dog. The friendly Old English sheepdog, and his successors, captured the affections of an audience interested in *them* at least as much as the paint they were promoting. Dash

Henry, the proud mum.

Dash arrives in style.

was the dog who held the Dulux fort for the first ten years, and when the time came for him to hang up his collar, a Rolls Royce delivered him to the Café Royal where he met the six finalists in a competition to find his successor. No fewer than 450 contestants had been tested for personality, temperament, grooming and behaviour. A clear winner was Fernville Lord Digby of Sheffield, who also took home £250, a silver feeding bowl and a year's supply of dog food. And just to make sure Digby didn't lose the contract, his owner, butcher Norman Harrison, took no chances when the two were travelling to the London TV studios where the commercials were filmed. The perfection of the wild, luxuriant hair that was Digby's trademark was protected from the elements by a special, bespoke hard-wearing topcoat (what else!). It also ensured that some of the first-class seats on the Inter-City express between Sheffield and London weren't covered rather more luxuriously than British Rail intended.

Ten years later, Digby had retired, and a third Old English sheepdog, Duke, was on TV duty – and revealing how he got

Digby, dressed to travel.

himself ready for his 'paint job'. Not for him the *haut-couture* shampoos preferred by some fancy dogs. Instead, a quick burst of washing up liquid was all he needed to send himself into a lather. Then his groom, Dawn Hutchinson, got to work with a brush and a hair dryer. The whole process took an entire morning, before Duke was ready to step into the stylish pawmarks of his distinguished predecessors.

Certainly the most intelligent dog to grace our TV screens in recent years is a delightful rascal of a mongrel called Pippin. About 14 inches tall, her parentage is uncertain, but she's thought to have some poodle, spaniel and Lhasa Apso in her. She is trained by Ann Head, who says 'she just loves to learn'. And it was that ability to pick up instructions that won Pippin a leading role in the children's TV programme 'Woof' with Liza Goddard. The magazine *Dogs Today* reported her wide range of tricks. 'She glides across your screen on a scooter, blows out candles on a birthday cake, and sits on a bridge, hoisting a bag of shopping up on the end of a rope'. Ann said: 'It took nine months to get the choreography for the rope trick right, but that wasn't intensive training. You don't want the dog to get bored and lose interest. Pippin likes variety just like the rest of us'. Which is why, no doubt, she has starred in pet food

WOOF!

FIDOMEET
VOICE
OVER

'She glides across your screen on a scooter.'

commercials shown in France and Italy, advertised videotapes in Germany and fronted the Belgian government's campaign to persuade motorists to use lead-free petrol. In addition she was voted Spain's TV Personality of the Year for her part in a series of public information broadcasts which required her to open, pack, close

Pippin in her many roles: delivering a petition to the South Koreans (above), with the famous short, fat, hairy legs of Ernie Wise (right) and as Mum, with two of her pups (above right).

and carry a suitcase, turn off a television set, tidy socks away in a drawer, play the piano and even play chess ('She doesn't know all the moves, but she can certainly manoeuvre the pieces round the board!').

Pippin's home is crowded with gold, silver and Grand Prix awards for her work in advertising. She teamed up with

In love with Phil Collins (below left), with chicks (below), and (bottom) with Richard Briers and the Thames Valley Police

actor Richard Briers to make a film for Thames Valley Police, warning children about the danger of talking to strangers; then got together with comedian Ernie Wise to make an anti-litter film for a Tidy Britain campaign; and was signed up to add a little long-haired glamour to the video of the Phil Collins hit 'Something Happened on the Way to Heaven'. Ann Head even persuaded her to be photographed with baby chicks climbing all over her head; and to deliver a letter to the South Korean embassy complaining about the way they treat dogs in their country. But Pippin's biggest and best production was the birth of seven magnificent puppies looking every bit a chip off the old block.

Instant celebrity status for Pickles who shows where he found the World Cup.

A black and white mongrel called Pickles acquired a flash of momentary stardom when he found football's missing World Cup in 1966. Pickles was out for a walk in the London suburb of Norwood with his owner, David Corbett, when he started sniffing and pawing at something wrapped in newspaper under a bush. Mr Corbett unwrapped the parcel and found himself holding the £30,000 cup that police forces throughout Britain and the continent had been hunting for.

He started sniffing and pawing at something wrapped in newspaper.

After that canine triumph, it was only right that the official mascot for the England team in the next World

74

Cup in 1970 should be a dog. But Winston, the British bulldog chosen for the role had to be replaced after developing a strong affection for his owner, Major George Lewis of Great Hallingbury in Essex. Winston – better known at Cruft's as Blockbuster Brevice August Moon – was to have gone to Mexico City a month before the kick-off to acclimatise himself to the 7,350ft altitude. But the Major decided that 'as Winston is a pet of the family, one of his pups will go instead'. The English Football Supporters' Association, which was subsidising Winston's trip, bravely

Winston, subsituted in the final squad for Mexico.

concealed any disappointment with the brief press statement: 'We thought it better that a younger dog should go'. But by the time the World Cup came round, all had been sorted out. Winston Junior had duly passed a fitness test, been insured for £50,000 and, when his official duties were over, was all set to become the pet of the British Ambassador in Mexico.

Lulu was in the habit of urinating on the guests' shoes

Possibly the most reviled dog in the diplomatic world was Lulu, lapdog to His Most Exceptional and Extraordinary Majesty Haile Selassie, Emperor of Ethiopia. The *Daily Mail* reported that one of the key functionaries at the Emperor's court was the Dog Man. His job was to shadow Lulu as the little brute mingled with VIPs during imperial audiences and receptions. He was assigned to that role because Lulu was in the habit of urinating on the guests' shoes, and protocol forbade any reaction – so the Dog Man repaired the damage with a satin napkin!

The Emperor and Lulu were in clear need of the great Barbara Woodhouse, who had a telepathic understanding of all aberrations in dog behaviour. Jumping up, for example, could, she said, be stopped by a sharp pull on a large choker chain. And in her BBC2 programme 'Training Dogs the Barbara Woodhouse Way', she demonstrated how to teach dogs the basic commands – sit, stay, lie down, come and wait – in just six minutes. Her own dog, Junia, often on film locations, would bark to order in response to her mistress blinking off set. Ten blinks – ten barks! The Woodhouse advice to the owners of the 17,000 dogs she actually trained was: 'Be fair, be firm, be fun'.

This was her summary of those ground rules:

'FAIR – Be consistent. Don't scold about something you have allowed before. Command clearly, with the dog's name first - "Fido come!" not "Come for Mummy!" 15 minutes training daily is adequate.

'FIRM – Start house-training at six weeks. I usually confine

Chase a dog and you lose your dignity.

a pup to an indoor kennel for three days, letting him outside to play and spend pennies. This builds up the right indoor/ outdoor association. Start lead-training by eight weeks; if the dog runs off, turn tail yourself – in the opposite direction. He'll soon catch up. Chase a dog and you lose your dignity. As for punishment, dogs respond to tones of voice: a severe one is often punishment enough.

'FUN – Be loving, quick to praise, playful. I race and wrestle with my dog – she loves it.'

And if all that fails, don't forget your satin handkerchief!

Barbara Woodhouse applies a firm hand.

BIONIC DOGS AND MEDICAL MOMENTS

Gwen, an eight-year-old sheepdog, helped her master to the title of Britain's Shepherd of the Year. Working in the rugged hills of Perthshire, the two of them nursed record production out of their 2000-strong flock. What made the achievement all the more praiseworthy was that Gwen had only three legs. George Reid, manager of the Lynmore Sheep Farm at Glenquaich, had been devastated when his hard-working dog broke a leg bringing sheep down from the hills. Normally, such a badly injured animal would be put down. Instead, George had her leg taken off at the shoulder, and slowly and painfully nursed her back to health. The plucky dog could no longer manage the harder tasks at the top of the hills but, 'She is', says George, 'a real wizard in the pens. I just don't know what I would do without her'.

Not all dogs are as adaptable as George to adverse circumstances, and their owners often go to remarkable lengths to keep their pets mobile. In 1984, Ben, a beer-loving terrier, slipped a disc, paralysing his hind quarters. Owner Roy Mottram didn't want him to miss his regular trips to their favourite pub in Hulme, just outside Manchester. So he spent £100 on a special two-wheeled cart to support the four-year-old terrier's back legs. Ben continued to enjoy his daily pint of beer, and Roy took the jibes about his 'legless' pet in his stride.

Harry Feakes of Timperley in Cheshire came up with a less

Ben considers how to tackle the second half-pint.

78

expensive solution when his eight-year-old Sealyham, Sam, trapped a nerve in his spine, paralysing his back legs. Harry converted his wife Clara's old shopping trolley to keep the little fellow moving. The device gave Sam a new turn of speed – although it was never quite explained what contortions he went into at lampposts.

Yet another kind of 'wheelchair' was dreamt up by vet's assistant Linda Blake in Egham in 1965, when she was confronted by Fido, a dog paralysed when his owner accidentally closed a door on him. Linda persuaded her engineer father to make a frame which just lifted Fido's rear legs off the ground. It gave his legs a chance to recover. The only problem was that when the time came to throw the contraption away, Fido didn't want to.

Left *Fido's frame.*

Had the inventors of these ingenious mechanical aids but known it, there was an even simpler solution – acupuncture. Judy the dachshund – incontinent, and with her legs

79

Bruno looks none too happy about his rejuvenating treatment.

virtually paralysed – appeared doomed. Then her owner, Hilda Brooking from Twickenham, heard of a vet who practised the oriental healing technique. A needle in the right place did the trick, and Judy was cured.

Bruno started receiving his acupuncture treatment after his 17th birthday in 1978. The mongrel was beginning to show signs of wear and tear, and was taken to Elizabeth Cadam's surgery in Lancashire. The acupuncture transformed him. Bruno was last heard of still going strong at the ripe old age of 22, which is around 154 in human terms. Since then the idea has grown in popularity. *Dogs Today* recently reported that 'many owners are now requesting acupuncture for their pets, because they have been treated successfully by it themselves. The anatomical points targeted are vital – corresponding to the particular ailments. Most vets use about 40, although very experienced practitioners may use up to 360 (compared to 1,000 possible sites on the human body). Sessions generally last for about 40 minutes, and must take place on a regular basis. The longer the treatment continues, the better the results – but it is heavy on your vet's time, and an appropriately heavy hole will appear in your bank balance. The placid dog is a more promising patient, and the treatment is said to be so relaxing that dogs often fall asleep.'

Wealthy widow Edith Lowy decided her dog Sam's back problems were so bad that she booked him into a clinic for humans. The pampered poodle was enrolled in a physiotherapy course at the exclusive Edgbaston

The placid dog is a more promising patient.

Clinic in Birmingham, where staff were more accustomed to dealing with the injuries of top sporting stars. But they didn't turn a hair when their new patient came in on all fours for his costly – and ultimately successful – heat treatment.

When her mongrel, Rex, lost one of his front paws in a road accident, 13-year-old Flora MacKenzie of Portsmouth thought he would never again be able to join in the ball games in the park which he loved so much. She reckoned without the help of a local surgical factory, which made and fitted an artificial paw, giving Rex back all his old speed and agility. That was back in 1955, but the idea was far from new. In 1932, Phyllis, a fox terrier owned by the Bidwell family of Birmingham, had her hind feet crushed by a lorry. An expert was called in to fit her with miniature replicas of human artificial limbs – long steel boots which gave the local cats plenty of warning of her approach.

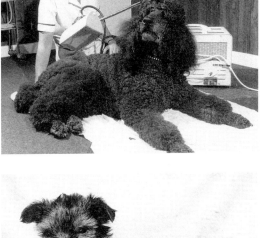

Top *Going private: Sam enjoys special attention at the Edgbaston Clinic.* Above *Peg-leg Pete.*

There was no need for experts as far as Pat Hughes of Liverpool was concerned. When her Yorkshire terrier, Pete, was born with a deformed leg, Pat waited until he was six weeks old, and then taped a clothes peg to the stump. The crafty crutch made sure Pete was level-pegging with other dogs when it came to walks in the park.

The pampered poodle was enrolled in a physiotherapy course.

Jon the Labrador's problem was that every time he went for a walk, he limped home on sore paws – the result of an allergy that made him a tenderfoot. His owner, Jennie Moore of Heaton Moor in Cheshire, paid a surgical bootmaker £12 to measure Jon up for a smart set of pigskin lace-ups. 'His paws never seemed to heal', said Jenny, 'and the boots seemed the only answer.' Passers-by – unaware of the medical problem – thought it was just the doggie equivalent of one-upmanship.

Another sight that would have prompted double-takes was Londoner Vera Appleton pushing her Samoyed dog, Susan, in a wheelchair in 1958. The paralysed pooch wasn't expected to live long, but the wheelchair gave Susan's limbs a chance of recovery. When last seen, she was defying the vet and taking a few tentative steps on her own again.

Passers-by thought it was just the doggie equivalent of one-upmanship.

No such luck for Sally, a Manchester terrier who suffered a heart attack. Destined never again to set paw to pavement, she was taken for her daily constitutional perched in an old wheelchair. Her owner, Marjorie

Sally (right) and Susan (far right) enjoy a breath of fresh air thanks to their dedicated owners.

Robinson-Newbauld, probably never considered major heart surgery as an alternative. Yet that was precisely what happened to Tootsie, a tiny Yorkshire terrier who fainted every time she got excited. Vets discovered that a major artery had narrowed, and gave Tootsie six months to live – unless she had surgery. During the two-hour operation at the Royal Veterinary College in Potters Bar, Hertfordshire, in 1984, Tootsie was given a blood transfusion from another dog called Sparky. The vets pronounced the operation successful, and said Tootsie should make a full recovery.

A tiny Yorkshire terrier who fainted every time she got excited.

By 1989, canine surgery was making even greater strides, and turned its attentions to Sophie, a young springer spaniel, who would suddenly pass out after she'd been running for a few minutes. The Dolan family from Dagenham took her along to their vet, who diagnosed that her heart was beating far too slowly. The tablets he prescribed failed to cure the problem – which was why Sophie found herself at Cambridge University Veterinary Hospital, having a human pacemaker fitted in a touch-and-go operation.

'We thought they were joking', said Chris Dolan. 'I mean, have you ever heard of a dog with a pacemaker?'

Then again, have you every heard of a dog with leukaemia? Probably not – this disease of the blood is very rare in the canine world. But in 1960 it was diagnosed in Candy, a 14-month-old Scottie owned by Hazel Pike of Hitchin in Hertfordshire. A vet said that only a blood transfusion could save the dog's life. Step forward Sheena, an Alsatian bitch who'd been taken to a local kennels to be put down. She duly provided a pint of blood which – along with a course of cortisone treatment – returned Candy to almost perfect health. Sheena had saved Candy's life – and her own too. The kennels decided that Sheena should

He quickly returned to full health after being fitted with a splendid set of dentures.

stick around just in case the Alsatian blood gave Candy any big ideas!

An RAF dog helping to guard Gibraltar airport in 1983 could have been put down when he broke a tooth. Instead a Navy dentist gave him a new one in white and yellow gold in a 15-minute operation. The *Sunday Mirror* duly recorded the surgeon's verdict: 'Alsatians are easier to work on than humans'. The idea caught on. Three years later, Gist, a German shepherd demonstration dog stopped eating when he broke a tooth and the stump became infected. Worried owner, Colin Tennant, arranged for Gist to be fitted with a gleaming gold fang.

Vets in France went one better, helping a terrier to put its bite back on equal terms with its bark. The unfortunate hound lost six teeth after being struck by a car near Verdun. He quickly returned to full health after being fitted with a splendid set of dentures. The only question – where did he put them at night?

Two dogs unlikely to have had need of a dentist were the dachshunds who belonged to Lady Ellis, wife of the scientist Sir Charles Ellis. In 1966 she was brushing their teeth twice a day at her home in Cookham Dean, Berkshire. The dogs – Katie and Jenny – seemed none too keen on the idea, but, as Lady Ellis explained: 'I believe regular brushing keeps a dog's teeth clean and healthy right into old age'. And she added: 'We've tried various toothpaste flavours, including vanilla, strawberry and banana; but they definitely prefer peppermint'. Lady Ellis was before her time. It was another quarter of a century before the top people's London store, Harrods, was telling dog owners they could look forward to fresh-smelling doggie breath with the help of a specially developed toothbrush and toothpaste. Just to prove the point, Sam the Irish setter was dragooned in to give an early morning demonstration of dental hygiene.

The little mongrel in a New York dog's home found the

perfect owner in 25-year-old Theresa Startthaus. Both of them were deaf, and Theresa taught the dog, Sharona, the usual commands in sign language. Clearly a case of love at first sight.

But the Pruskin family didn't discover their Dalmatian puppy Misty was deaf until after they bought her. It took them 18 months to teach her the ropes. A wag of the finger saw her obediently 'sit'; a sweeping gesture of the hand meant lie down; and a patted leg meant 'heel'.

The Bostick family of Port Washington, New York, first realised that Randy, their nine-year-old Bedlington terrier, had gone deaf when he stopped barking at the door bell. Not for them the painstaking chore of teaching their pet sign language. Randy was fitted with a hearing aid – with the battery strapped

Randy gets used to his hearing aid.

to a harness on his back – and was speedily back in business, barking at all callers.

The cure for Sonia Rankin's boxer dog, Kim, was a large ice-pack. Sonia mixed brandy, wine, rum and orange juice into a special bowl for a party at her home in Wylam, Northumberland. Then she popped out to do some last-minute shopping, and while she was away Kim swigged the lot. Sonia returned to find her pet pegged out under the kitchen table, absolutely legless. It took two days of tender care, nursing – and ice-packs – to bring the hung-over hound back to the land of the living. (It was thought that hair of the dog might be a touch tactless). And the incident gave a whole new meaning to the phrase 'punch-drunk boxer'.

A fashion parade for 200 dogs in London in 1956 was unexpectedly dominated by a handsome little wire-haired fox terrier called Whiskey, who came along to watch, but ended up stealing the show. Tugging and barking beside her mistress, she seemed to think that she would make a much more interesting exhibit on the 'dog-walk'. She was right! For 'she' used to be a 'he'. Her owner, Laurie Minchin of Wimbledon, explained that Whiskey had had a sex change operation: 'Not that it has harmed her. She's enjoyed this party and seems the gayest dog of them all'.

Putting your pet on the pill is pretty routine now – but one of the first dogs to try out the new contraceptive when it first came on the market in 1969 was a London poodle called Lori Merrymorn. Her first confrontation with the pill was not exactly a howling success. She stared at it, sniffed at it, stalked around it, and turned her nose up at it, before finally being persuaded to give it a try.

Facing page
Sonia Rankin shows concern for her hung-over hound.

While she was away Kim swigged the lot.

Lori the poodle examines the pill.

Benson the mongrel had no such doubts. But the 'pills' he turned out to have eaten were rather larger. Vets didn't discover what they were until a distinctly off-colour Benson was whipped into their surgery for a medical examination. An X-ray revealed five conkers, which were duly removed during a special operation at the RSPCA hospital in Putney. All concerned expressed the hope that Benson would now bone up on what dogs are supposed to have for dinner.

The guidance would have benefited Paul Worrow's Labrador, Henry, as well. While helping four-year-old Paul to play garages, Henry playfully consumed a model of a Ford GT racing car. He was rushed to a hospital run by the People's Dispensary For Sick Animals, where a vet, using long instruments, managed to reverse the car out of him.

The business of having puppies (as opposed to cars or conkers) can cause sleeplessness in dogs. With some, it is so persistent that without a surgical operation, they would not survive the births. Countess Christina Hardenberg, a non-medical practitioner from Uelzen, near Hamburg, found an easier solution in 1977. She took to swinging a brass pendulum across the dogs' eyes until they started to yawn and fall asleep.

A vet, using long instruments, managed to reverse the car out of him.

Another new medical phenomenon that emerged during the 1970s was the dog psychologist. One of the first was Dr John Kernell, who set up a canine consulting room couch in San Francisco, and was worked off his feet by a steady stream of dog lovers and their hung-up pets. Many of his cases seemed more in need of a marriage guidance counsellor – like the tearful bride who came in for advice about her Alsatian. The jealous dog apparently lay in wait for its new master, and attacked him when he came home from work. 'The answer was simple', said Dr Kernell. 'I advised the new husband to kiss the dog before he kissed his new bride. Now the dog adores him as much as the bride does.' Dr Kernell reckoned that the increasingly hectic pace of life was to blame for neuroses in dogs as well as humans. Which could explain why he went on to set up the world's first course in dog psychology at a Californian university. Privately, the doctor reckoned that most of his students would eventually find themselves treating more owners than dogs.

In 1985 a dog psychiatrist stepped in to save an Alsatian sentenced to death by magistrates in Sussex. They'd decided two-year-old Gemma had to be destroyed

A Doberman explains the problem to Dr Kernell.

after she mauled another dog, leapt up at a pensioner and trapped a terrified milkman in his float. Gemma's heartbroken owners appealed against the verdict, and called in pet therapist, Harry Carter. First he took the Alsatian to a hospital's geriatric ward to get her used to meeting old folk (they gave her a great welcome). Then he took her to a milk depot where she was fussed over by a milkman. After the treatment, Harry's report was handed to a judge at Chichester Crown Court. She was so impressed she lifted the death sentence – on the condition that Gemma attended obedience classes.

It would take an army of psychiatrists to attend the hundreds of thousands of dogs who bite someone, somewhere, each year. Research suggests that at least 480 dog bites are reported for every 100,000 people. On top of that, joggers and cyclists receive many bites which go unreported. In Britain, 7,000 postmen were attacked in 1989; 500 of the cases ended up in court. The largest single difficulty the Post Office has is proving ownership.

The National Canine Defence League thought it had the answer way back in 1939, when it issued dog 'passports' -

"I advised the new husband to kiss the dog before he kissed his new bride."

identification cards with their own special wallet, which also contained a photograph, licence and pedigree. In the first rush of enthusiasm, thousands were applied for, but the scheme never took off on a mass scale; and it was clear that for it to be really successful, *every* dog owner had to do it.

Passport control for two dogs at the National Canine Defence League.

France and Austria solved the problem in 1970 when they made the marking and registration of dogs compulsory. That same year saw the launching of a British Dog Registry in anticipation of a similar law being passed in Britain. To that end the Dog Registry spent a great deal of time, money and research in perfecting a clinically-acceptable instrument that imprinted a number - subcutaneously, indelibly and painlessly - on the inner side of a dog's hind leg.

The United States followed suit in 1977 with the Earmark Registry, which involved a 'lifetime identification mark' being tattooed on dogs' ears. Special tattoo clinics were set up for the operations, which were also said to be completely painless. The mark was then registered at a central bureau so that a dog could be identified on request. The system proved invaluable in tracing strays and discouraging thefts.

However, successive British and American governments have drawn back from imposing a legally enforceable universal registration system - even though a British RSPCA survey in 1988 showed that 92 per cent of the population wanted one. A series of savage dog attacks on children led to the setting up of a limited registration system for certain dangerous breeds in 1991 – and the contract for administering that went to a charity which only three years earlier had launched its own National Pet

Register. From its Hertfordshire headquarters, the Wood Green Animal Shelter aims to reunite lost pets with their owners throughout the United Kingdom. So far it has built up details of more than 100,000 pets, 85 per cent of which are dogs.

The NPR is manned 24 hours a day, 365 days a year by specially trained operators – not answering machines. This makes sure that anyone finding or losing an animal which is on the Register receives instant response, personal service and immediate action.

Tattooing is also available, along with freeze branding and transponder implants.

Once an animal is registered (cost – £8, including third party liability for the first year), the details of the owner's name, address and the animal's description are entered on a computer for the lifetime of the pet. Subsequent changes of address – or even when the animal is staying with friends or on holiday – can also be entered. A unique identity in the form of an engraved disc is provided, but the American option of tattooing is also available, along with freeze branding and transponder implants. (They have not yet got round to the idea offered since 1989 in Uruguay, where dogs are issued with ID cards containing not only their photographs, but their noseprints as well!).

One telephone call to the National Pet Register's fully computerised system will identify the owner of a pet immediately. It is an ambitious project, with the capacity to store details of no fewer than 80,000,000 pets.

It could quickly and easily adapt itself to run a compulsory register, should the government decide to introduce one. And then tracking down any dog with dentures, a pacemaker, a hearing aid, a gold tooth or a wooden leg would presumably be no problem at all!

AMAZING FEATS

Dogs can be trained to do many things, but a rare few have abilities that stretch far beyond normal expectations. Most self-respecting canines would do their best to summon a bark if a stranger came into their house. Not Princess Jacqueline! This bulldog would welcome visitors with a cheery 'Hello', and speed parting guests on their way with a polite 'Call again'. In the 1930s, Jacqueline – owned by Mrs Mabel Robinson, of Waterville in Maine – was believed to be the only dog in the world who could imitate human speech. Noted for her social graces, she apparently understood the meaning of what she said – and her vocabulary ran to around 20 words. Unlike parrots, the dog showed a clear understanding of the distinction between 'I will' and 'I won't'; and there was no mistaking her request in plain English to be 'let out'. Jacqueline's throat was examined by Dr Knight Dunlap of John Hopkins University, who revealed that, in addition to her normal canine 'noise box', she possessed vocal chords remarkably similar to those of human beings. Her most ambitious word gave away this bulldog's easy lifestyle – it was 'elevator'.

Ben, another talking dog, from Royston in Hertfordshire, was rather more limited in his attempts at conversation. In fact, he could manage only one phrase – 'I want one'! Nevertheless, in 1946, the BBC decided that the potential for an interesting conversation was there, and sent round 'a team of interviewers and engineers' to record Ben for posterity. Mr Stephen Grenfell, who conducted the interview, relayed its contents to the *Daily Mirror*:

The potential for an interesting conversation was there.

Mr Grenfell: Well, Ben, have you any puppies?
Ben: I want one.

Mr Grenfell: If you want puppies, Ben, the first thing is to get a wife.

Ben: I want one.

Mr Grenfell: What do you think of the political situation, Ben?

Ben: I want one.

Their somewhat unproductive chat at least gave the Mirror the chance to come up a classic tabloid headline – 'DOG TELLS BBC HE WANTS A WIFE'.

In 1951, Peter the puppy astounded his owner, Mrs Field of West Croydon, by saying 'please' when he wanted a dog biscuit. Holding out a biscuit just out of his reach,

Peter, the dog who learned the magic word.

Peg gives the answer to the Italian press.

in the hope that he might speak a little more, she said 'Please what?' 'Mum,' replied Peter; and Mrs Field recalled that Peter had first said 'Mum' some months earlier when he wanted his bandaged paw attended to. The 11-month-old mongrel had clearly identified the magic word that got an instant

response for the children of the house – and reckoned it might just produce the same result for him!

The Italian press went appropriately berserk in 1957 over a poodle named Peg who made herself understood by picking out letters of the alphabet with her teeth. The letters of the Italian alphabet from A to Z were stamped in black on white celluloid squares about the size of postcards. Peg could also choose from cards numbered in Arabic figures from 0 to 9. A ribbon was threaded through a hole in the corner of each card, and the clever dog compiled

words by picking up letter cards in the right order. She was even able to copy words underlined in a newspaper, and would occasionally show her affection for her mistress, Mrs Ines Corridori, by spelling out 'Darling Ines' or 'Dear Ines'. Peg was also said to be capable of simple arithmetic. One normally cynical journalist who observed the poodle in action was moved to write: 'It really is a remarkable phenomenon, able to convince even the most sceptic and diffident person'.

Then there was Patch, a cross-corgi who was dumped from a car when she was a pup, and grew up to become what other dogs would regard as a mathematical genius. Her master, 65-year-old George Bailey, invited the press into his home in Preston in 1976 to test his pet's sums. 'We asked: "What is four minus one?" Three barks was the response. "How many pennies?" we asked, producing a ten pence piece. Ten barks. We showed her a three of hearts playing card and an ace of diamonds. Three barks and one bark. She added a further bark to indicate they were red cards – it's five barks for black cards. Then George set the hands of the clock to five. Patch gave five barks. We admitted defeat and left! '

Patch has no trouble with this simple addition.

Ten years later, a cocker spaniel called Ebony was laying

When the biscuits ran out, so did his mathematical abilities.

claim to being the doggie mastermind of all time. Aided and abetted by journalist Colin Wills, Ebony's skills were said to embrace adding, subtracting, multiplying and dividing. There was, however, a hint of the spaniel's secret technique. He was apparently bribed with ginger nuts, which perhaps meant that when the biscuits ran out, so did his mathematical abilities.

Step up the Barking and Houndsditch

In return for a biscuit or two, Ebony poses for the cameras

A little bitchiness caused by puppy love amongst the young choristers.

Choral Society! You're right – they were all singing dogs, and they played a major role in the making of a 1972 record called 'Queen of the Alley Dogs'. Rehearsals were reported to have gone well, 'marred only by a little bitchiness caused by puppy love among the young choristers – but, for all that, the disc was expected to be a howling success'.

A miner from Clowne in Derbyshire laid claim to the world's first animal answerphone. Telephone callers were greeted by the sound of Nigel Newstead's thirteen-year-old poodle, Roger, 'wuffling and barking into the receiver' after the dog had first picked it up and

All eyes on the conductor at the recording session.

'It's for you!'

dropped it on the carpet. 'I've lost count of the number of times I've rushed into the room to find Roger barking at some mystified caller,' said Nigel. Roger's fixation with the phone started as a puppy when he took a disliking to the ringing tone. It took him only a short while to learn how to make the ringing stop. So every time the phone rings in the Newstead household there is a frantic dash by Nigel and his wife Valerie to reach it before Roger does.

The warning didn't reach Mrs Janis McLeod, from Wallasey on Merseyside, who devoted much time and energy to teaching her dog, Emma, to answer

It took him only a short while to learn how to make the ringing stop.

the telephone. The six-year-old Lhasa Apso was already an old hand at strolling along pushing a baby cart, putting litter in the bin, dancing and closing doors. Emma's performances won her the title of 'Most Talented Dog in Great Britain' in 1990, as well as that of 'Top Dog' in a National Canine Defence League Competition sponsored by the magazine *Dogs Today*.

Savage, a mongrel with a thoroughbred brain, had won more than 400 prizes for obedience when Mrs Lesley Scholes locked herself out of her Hampshire holiday cottage, leaving the key in the inside lock. It didn't take long for Savage to claw it out of the keyhole, pick it up in his mouth, and pass it to his mistress through the letterbox as she held it open. Said Mrs Scholes, 'I knew Savage was intelligent, but this takes the biscuit'.

Dogs Today sought the answer to canine cleverness from Ann Head, owner and trainer of media star, Pippin (see page 71). She explained why she regarded training dogs as 'programming the computer'. 'You must start when they are young – their minds are like blotting paper at that stage. If they were in the wild, their mothers would be teaching them survival. In comparison, a domestic dog's brain lies fallow. Giving a dog something to think about is a wonderful thing, and a bored dog can become a destructive dog.'

Animal behaviourist Peter Neville agrees: 'Most dogs could probably just manage "sit", "lie" and "roll over", merely because their owners don't – or can't – spend any time teaching new things. Dogs helping disabled people in America must obey a minimum of 90 commands. However, once you start defining a dog's reasoning in human terms, it starts to get a bit dodgy. He may be making certain signals, but we just don't know for sure how dogs think!

That didn't stop *Dogs Today* from linking up with Mensa, the society for people of very high intelligence, to devise an IQ test for dogs. Britain's canniest canines were served notice that

*Savage shows
how he saved his
mistress from an
embarassing
situation.*

running for a stick or fetching slippers was no longer good enough. They had to be judged on their success rate with five tough tests.

Test One

Take a dog's two favourite toys and show them to him. When he takes one, describe it with a short word. When he takes the second, describe it with a second word. Repeat five times. Place toys before the dog. Ask him to pick up a particular one. He should go straight for it. If he doesn't move, he – and possibly you – have got problems!

Running for a stick or fetching slippers was no longer good enough.

Test Two

Place cheese in front of your dog. Say cheese and let him eat it. Repeat test. Put cheese on floor again, but lead dog into next room. Wait one minute, say cheese and release dog. He should go straight to it – and probably eat it. If he has to be shown the cheese again, he's a dunce!

Test Three

Show cheese to the dog. Then hide it when he's not looking. Say cheese, and release him nearby. Top marks if he finds it within 30 seconds. Bottom marks if he loses interest!

The scores are charitably doubled for bloodhounds, beagles, boxers, bull mastiffs, bull terriers and bassets.

Test Four

Tether dog and give him a treat. Tie second treat to a piece of string. Place treat within his reach, and tell him to get it with his paw. Repeat with treat out of reach but end of string within reach. Award him major brownie points if he gets the treat within 30 seconds. If he doesn't get it, even when you help out by placing the string under his paw – or gives up and barks – you know you're on to a loser.

Test Five

Construct maze with furniture. Place cheese at end of maze. Say 'cheese' and lead dog through maze to treat. Praise him. Repeat without giving him any help.

The exam included handicaps for different breeds. Border collies should be able to perform their tasks in half the allotted time. The scores are charitably doubled for bloodhounds, beagles, boxers, bull mastiffs, bull terriers and bassets. The *Daily Mail* decided to put a random selection of dogs through the tests. Not all were cheese lovers, so chocolate biscuits were substituted. The lowest score, surprisingly, went to Joey, a border collie cross; the best, with almost full marks, was Lulu, a springer spaniel.

Vet and columnist Dr Bruce Fogle gave his verdict: 'The tests are basically fun for adult dogs, but in puppies up to eight weeks old, they could actually be beneficial for both mental and physical development. Doing tests like these can actually make dogs' brains grow bigger'.

But perhaps the best judgement came from MP David Blunkett, whose guide dog sits with him in the House of Commons: 'Most of the people judged to be highly intelligent I have found are as thick as puddings when it comes to life. Dogs may have the same traits'.

HOUNDS GET AROUND

Dogs used to get around fine on their own four paws –
until friendly humans came along with helping hands that
come in shapes and sizes which lazier hounds find quite
irresistible.   At one extreme, an expensive, up-market
The surprising   handbag specially designed to carry smaller pets in
sight of Kelly and   complete safety, and launched by actress Katie Boyle and
Maxi out for a   her two Pekingese in 1962; at the other, the back-seat
drive.   barkers – at their most splendid in the shape of Maxi, an

Old English sheepdog, and Kelly, an Irish wolfhound anxious to prove that even sitting down he was still the tallest dog in Britain (see page 30). In a 1974 open-topped Triumph Herald, the two pals clearly appreciated not having to stick their heads out of the window to catch the slipstream.

Some owners are reluctant to allow their dogs to roam all over the family car, and banish them to a 'cage' at the back, where they can be seen, heard – and smelt – without the inconvenience of them leaping and moulting all over the passengers and driver. Very handy if you have an estate car – rather more difficult if you own a saloon. The Japanese attempted to crack this problem in 1966, when a Tokyo factory produced an appliance called the 'Transcage', which allowed dogs to breath when carried in the *boot*. Adaptable to any make of car, it consisted of a chrome strip, perforated with large airholes, running round between the rear edge of the boot and the partly-closed lid. That idea was stylishly put in the shade by Ernie Todd of Victoria, British Columbia, who fitted a couple of ship's portholes in the top of his car boot so that hounds Tyee and Skeeter could sniff that fresh Pacific air while accompanying

Eyes left. Tyee and Skeeter spot something interesting from their unique vantage point.

him on his travels. Ernie even took the added precaution of measuring the dogs' heads and necks, and cutting portholes to match – one was eight inches in diameter, the other seven. After a couple of test runs, the dogs automatically homed in on the boot when they saw Ernie heading for

Each dog's head unerringly popped up through the right aperture.

the car and, after being safely locked in, each dog's head unerringly popped up through the right aperture. Samuel Beckett would have been proud of them!

A 'Dogs' Bus', which made its debut in Tokyo in 1968, was specially adapted to carry dogs and their owners from the city to a favourite summer resort in the foothills of Mount Fuji. The seats down one side of the aisle had been taken out

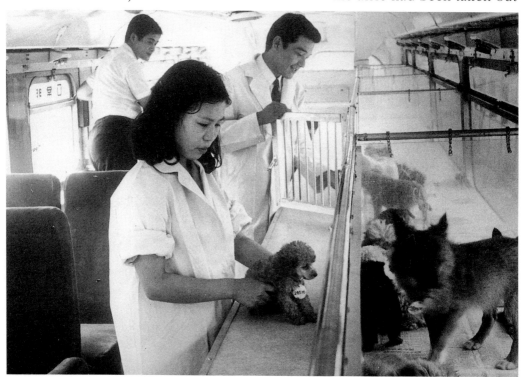

Holiday transport for Japanese dogs.

and replaced by a row of air-conditioned glass cages for the animals. The owners were allocated seats opposite their pets, so that each dog could see its master or mistress, and wouldn't panic during the journey. For added reassurance, attendants were on hand to make sure every canine need was catered for.

The only reassurance Mandy the Jack Russell needed was a pair of firm shoulders. Whenever 68-year-old Ray Roche set out for a spin on his bicycle, he knew that Mandy wouldn't be skipping alongside like normal dogs. Instead, Ray would stop his bicycle beside the garden shed, wait for Mandy to shin up a ladder to the roof – and step onto his shoulders. There she stayed, taking a balanced view of the world as Ray cycled down to the shops at Quedgeley in Gloucestershire.

Attendants were on hand to make sure every canine need was catered for.

A familiar sight in Egham, Surrey, during the 1950s was a retriever called Sally, proudly riding up front in the wicker basket that preceded a strange turn-of-the-century machine. It was an 1898 four-wheeler motorcycle known as a Beeston Quad, whose frame and two-and-three-quarter horse power engine had been painstakingly reconditioned by a Mr Williamson, director of a local garage. He kept the contraption in daily use, and Sally was his constant passenger – delighting in what she clearly thought was a new dog basket.

Bruce the Airedale terrier preferred to bring up the rear. His favourite travelling position was in a home-made two-wheel trailer towed by 'chauffeur' Bram

Above *Mandy goes for a ride.*
Left *Vintage transport for Sally.*

105

Pashley from Wakefield in Yorkshire. In 1969, Bram was cycling 30 miles a day with Bruce in tow, never tempted to jump out. 'I started training him as a passenger when he was a pup,' said Bram. 'Now I don't know which of us enjoys it most.'

Wheelies took over from walkies again in Seaford, Sussex, when John Anderson demonstrated the new device he'd patented for those who like to be in tandem with their pets. Complete with a see-through cover for instant, roll-down protection from the rain, this detachable platform on wheels was the final proof that people often lavish far more care on their pets than they do on themselves.

Inevitably, for a few dogs, the leisurely pace of a bicycle is simply not enough. Some prefer the hairier experience of riding a more powerful machine. In 1980, Mog the mongrel went goggle-eyed with delight when 21-year-old Sue Maddock fitted an old box to the back of her bike so he could travel to and from work with her. Sue, a farm-

hand from Stroud in Gloucestershire, had only one complaint: 'I would like him to have a crash helmet,' she said, 'but I haven't been able to find one small enough'. A quick spin down the road to Newbury in Berkshire might have found

Variations on a theme, and varying degrees of comfort for Bruce (facing page), Mog (left) and (above) John Anderson's elegant unnamed model.

Sam preferred the driving seat to riding pillion.

An eager Sam heads for the pub.

the headgear she was after. Charles Marshall had no difficulty tracking down a full set of Snoopy-type protection for Sam, his four-year-old motorcycling spaniel. Sam preferred the driving seat to riding pillion – which must have given passing motorists a nasty turn – especially if they'd known that master and pooch were heading down to the Black Bird Inn at Bagnor for some refreshment after a hard day's work on the farm. But Charles always made sure

Sam got home safely – or was it the other way round?

After all that, there are probably a growing number of dogs who have had enough of human ingenuity, and would prefer to go it alone in what they must see as an increasingly dangerous world. They could do worse than pad off to a shop in Coventry, where, for £19 a set, they could buy 'Rebark' trainers 'to give their paws extra bounce'!

Or, as the final, desperate line of defence, what about a bullet-proof vest, introduced at a hunting exhibition in Paris in 1985 by the French company SEMA, who were alarmed at the increasing number of dogs wounded by gunshots.

On second thoughts, it's clearly safer to stick to the roads!

Gun-dog preservation outfit.

THIS SPORTING LIFE

Below Hardly a racing start for this competitor in the Zurich swimming-dog race.
Below right Batsmen and fielders try to persuade Skye to part with his lastest find.

Most dogs love water, but few enter it in as dignified and gentlemanly a way as the unidentified swimmer taking the plunge at a canine competition in Zurich. With a helping hand from his owner, he seemed to be starting the dog paddle before he'd even hit the water.

No such encouragement was necessary for Skye, a springer spaniel that proved to be the most reliable fielder at Cholmondeley Cricket Club in Cheshire. He patrolled a nearby lake waiting for the sixes which regularly soared his way. And every time the ball hit the water, he dived in to retrieve it. His owner, club skipper Mark Ryland, said 'he saves us a fortune... the only trouble is getting the ball back from him afterwards'.

The mere ball has, of late, been replaced in some canine affections by the frisbee. And so popular has the sport become

in the USA that they often stage disc-catching competitions for dogs during breaks in major baseball games. Pepper Nichols of Wichita Falls, Texas, made the front pages as his dog Chino intercepted a frisbee during the Ashley Whippet Invitational World Championships, which provided extra entertainment for the capacity crowd watching the Washington Redskins' game at RFK Stadium in 1986.

Goal-keeping distraction at Highbury.

Some dogs aren't content to be part of a sideshow - they want to be in the main game itself. British soccer is littered with tales of dogs who hold up play by trying to get in on the act. In 1951 the Fulham goalkeeper took his eye off the ball to remove a stray that interrupted a key game with Arsenal at Highbury. And was another stray responsible for Milwall holding Spurs to a goalless draw in the third round of the FA Cup in 1967? There were plenty who argued about that. And about a controversial goal in a local league encounter in Rotherham, South Yorkshire. Tony Hunt, playing for the Brampton Dynamos, took a 20-yard shot at goal, and was amazed and delighted to see the ball deflected into the net off the head of a stray dog which had been busy watering the goalpost. The referee, rather unsportingly, played the offside rule, and disallowed the goal, which would have given the Dynamos victory. Their assistant manager, Les Walker, admitted 'we'd have been delighted to sign up the dog, but it did a runner'.

The highlight of a goalless draw at Milwall.

The scruffy mongrel that joined in a Staffordshire Sunday Cup match was somewhat luckier. He ran from the

touchline, intercepted the ball and brought the crowd to its feet with a flying header. Despite protests from Newcastle players, the referee, John Hilditch, allowed the goal. Knave of Clubs secretary David Hall confessed: 'It was the most amazing thing I have ever seen. A shot from one of our forwards was going wide when the dog dashed across the pitch and headed it back into the goal'.

The dog dashed across the pitch and headed it back into the goal.

In the face of such enthusiasm, it is hardly surprising that dogs would eventually get their own football games, unhindered by human players. The first such match was staged in 1950 at the Hagenbeck Zoo in Hamburg, when Lamp-post Wanderers met Boxers United in the Canine Cup. Both teams were reported to be well matched, with the ball the only bone of contention. Wanderers proved a little faster on the wings (they used greyhounds), but were weak in defence, where a poodle was substituting at left back. The all-boxer team of United were clever with both head

112

and feet (many of the forwards kicked with all four), and deservedly won 1-0, despite a tendency to give the referee a sharp nip in the ankle whenever he missed an infringement.

Perhaps Wanderers could have done with some help from a rather stylish papillon called Ricky, who walked on his front paws. Owned by pensioner Nora Lewis since he was a 12-week-old pup, Ricky was still entertaining the residents of Westwood, Peterborough with his party piece six years later.

Some dogs clearly feel life has dealt them an inappropriate hand of cards - a few set out to do something about it. The 1961 Epsom Spring meeting revealed the dog that would have preferred to be a racehorse. He took to the course with enthusiasm, and was still going strong when he passed the winning post soon after the finish of the Warren Stakes - to the great amusement of onlookers who searched in the form-book for this late entry in vain.

Jed completes a clear round.

Jed the Alsatian preferred showjumping. He amazed judges and spectators at a horse show at Creeting in Suffolk by jumping eight 2ft 6in fences in superb style. His owner, Janette Miller, had entered him as a joke, and was proud and delighted when he completed the course.

POOPER SCOOPERS

The Swiss have long expected their dogs to fall in line with the fastidious behaviour they demand of themselves. The spending of canine pennies on Zurich streets is unthinkable in daylight, and even at dead of night undertaken by only a desperate few. But in 1957, the city's burghers decided it was time to be more accommodating to their four-legged friends as they went about their business. They set aside an inviting lawn complete with a special welcome poster bearing the inscription 'YOU MAY DO IT HERE'. And to avoid any misinterpretation, 'it' was graphically explained by an accompanying illustration – just for the benefit of those dogs unable to read. The idea was developed further a year later in Frankfurt, when an enterprising citizen attempted to divert dogs away from some of the city's

Swiss discipline for dogs.

lamp posts – mainly the ones outside his business. Sadly, few could find the WC indicated on the signs (there were rumours it never existed), and were usually forced to unburden themselves by another lamp post further down the street.

Dog owners should install lamp posts in their garden.

By 1968, it was clearly time for a change of tactics. Antique dealer Graham Fuller, from Kedington in Suffolk, understood that lamp posts are one of the things that make a dog's life worth living. But he didn't see why dogs should have to walk the streets to sample their

An embarrassment of riches: Graham Fuller's dog doesn't know where to start.

delights. So he tried to market the idea that dog owners should install lamp posts in their garden. Not surprisingly, the idea didn't take off. But it was a good try – especially for an antique dealer stuck with a load of 50 railway surplus lamp posts!

So – back to square one – and perhaps the moment for Britain to build its versions of the 'dog lavatories' which, by the late Sixties, were multiplying rapidly throughout Europe. Among those first off the mark in the UK was Eastbourne councillor, Brian Williams, proudly described by his local paper as 'the brain behind the scheme'. He successfully campaigned to have one built in the town's Gildredge Park. Made of concrete blocks, it was 18 inches high, filled with sand and ashes,

Digby prefers not to perform in public.

It was left to a passing stray to casually christen the splendid structure.

and came complete with appropriate signpost. Four years later, the London Borough of Kensington and Chelsea jumped aboard the band-wagon, earmarking key sites for these modern 'doggie developments'. Hordes of distinguished press photographers jostled in expectation as television personality Robert Robinson led Digby, a Pyrenean mountain dog, up to the new convenience, to perform what passed for the opening ceremony. But Digby – a dog of some breeding – became rather embarrassed by all the

onlookers, and it was left to a passing stray to casually christen the splendid structure.

A more personalised variation on this theme was on offer from Hanover inventor Gerhard Bartels at the 1977 Nuremberg Inventors' Fair. His dog WC, complete with tree-stump, was designed for installation in a bathroom. Sales haven't exactly rocketed!

A plastic tree-stump doesn't have the same appeal.

A Karlsruhe owner hunts for 20 pfennigs.

Rather more successful were the vending machines positioned at strategic points around the German city of Karlsruhe in 1978. Dogs were allowed to ease themselves on the sidewalks provided their owners came armed with a 50 pfennig coin (20 pence).

His dog WC, complete with tree-stump, was designed for installation in a bathroom.

Inserted in one of the machines, it bought a cleansing set which consisted of a paper bag, a mini shovel and a scraper, both made of cardboard. The pooper scooper had arrived!

New York's city council thought it a

Any excuse for a photocall – pooper-scooping politicians in New York.

great idea and, that same year, hauled in leading local politicians to demonstrate the variety of devices the city's dog-owners were to be encouraged to use. With ordinances against fouling footpaths and sidewalks being passed in towns and cities across the United States, San Francisco jeweller, Sidney Mobell, designed his own upmarket pooper scooper, known as the 'poochie'. On sale at a mere $4,000, it came complete with a gold plate on which the owner's (or the pet's) name was spelled out in diamonds. Inevitably, it was available for Christmas: 'Darling – just what I've always wanted!' The pooper scooper as a status symbol had really arrived.

One year later, Portofino became the first city in Italy to require dog owners to clean up after their pets in public places. Hundreds of posters went up around the luxury resort spelling out the new law. The picture was endearing – the caption blunt: 'Soiling public places prohibited. Dog owners must remove their own animal's excrement. Scoopers and bags are provided free near city garbage disposal bins.'

Italian dog-owners get the message.

"I proprietari dei cani sono obbligati à rimuovere gli escrementi dei propri animali"

It was time for the Nuremberg Inventors' Fair to push forward the boundaries once again. Their 1981 displays included 'a portable toilet which can be strapped onto a dog'. We won't go into too much detail, but it was hardly designed to bring a smile to your pet's face!

Given a choice, most dogs would probably vote for Max Ponce's electronic 'Caninet', introduced in

'A portable toilet
which can be
strapped onto
a dog.'

Clermont-Ferrand in the spring of '83. An ultrasonic sound, inaudible to humans, attracts the pets to a sliding, horizontal surface set in the pavement. Quite how the dog is persuaded to relieve itself at that particular spot is not fully explained – but

*French plumbing
for dogs.*

when it has, an automatic machine flushes the droppings into the sewer system and disinfects the surface ready for the next visitor. One assumes – indeed hopes – that the machine has a way of knowing when the dog has finished.

Meanwhile, Paris – its dog population growing ever more numerous and wayward – was celebrating the arrival of the *mobile* pooper scooper. City officials launched a fleet of motorbikes, fully equipped with automatic brushes and hydraulic lifts. The drivers had simply to manoeuvre their vehicles into the right

position, press a button and, before you could say Jack Russell, the offending deposit had disappeared into a disposable bag.

Six years later, the Parisian cleansing department's technology had moved on. The motorcyclists of the 'Trottoirnet' patrolled with military precision, armed with vacuum guns, which gave them an opportunity to both speed up their operations and reach into the most unlikely and inaccessible places. Their turnover increased dramatically, with each driver managing between 400 and 600 'pick-ups' a day.

The 'Trottoirnet' patrolled with military precision, armed with vacuum guns.

Inspired by such a track record, Amsterdam invested in six similar mobile excrement removers. While Strasbourg, with 30,000 dogs on its streets, decided it needed the greater carrying capacity of three-wheeled bikes – which were also an added insurance against

Pooper patrol in Paris (right) and (facing page) in Hamburg (top) and Amsterdam (bottom).

careless drivers falling off into you-know-what.

No bikes in Hamburg – all the technology here went into the street vacuum cleaning equipment, which had to be guided around by someone on foot. That was until Frank Aubert turned up, and proved that this pooper scooper could be operated with some style –

*High-speed
scooping in
Hamburg.*

*Pippin shows
how to keep
Westminster tidy.*

if you wore roller skates!

All this was being carefully monitored by Westminster City Council in the heart of London. February, 1989,

This pooper scooper could be operated with some style – if you wore roller skates!

saw the introduction of its new by-law imposing a £100 fine on dog owners who refused to clean up after their pets had fouled a pavement. The clean-up campaign was launched by the comedian Bernie Winters and his St Bernard, Schnorbitz. Law-abiding owners were offered a wide choice of devices for collecting what a dog has to do. The Whoopsie Kit, the Scoop D Poop, Mess Mates and the Doggie Toilet all involved the use of a plastic bag. But Westminster's main weapon was the K-Nine Terrier, whose vacuum cleaner was so strong it really did remove without trace what the promotional literature delicately referred to as 'piles'.

A wide choice of devices for collecting what a dog has to do.

Of course, all these splendid machines and equipment would be put out of business if a French invention catches on. The Canicat is the first fully self-contained lavatory

for dogs – and cats. It was advertised as 'eliminating the need for an early morning walk', and is the size of a standard washing machine. It runs on electricity, and needs to be plumbed into the water supply too.

The only problem – perhaps it looks *too* much like a washing machine – and the problems if your pet happens to pop in through the wrong door simply don't bear thinking about!

A willing volunteer tries out the Canicat, but the cat looks less inclined to follow.

HEROIC DEEDS

The memorial to Barry, the original mountain rescuer.

Carved in stone, with a child clinging to his back, the memorial to the greatest canine hero of them all dominates the famous dog cemetery at Asnières, near Paris. 150 years ago his exploits in the Swiss mountains became the stuff of legend – the standard by which other such heroes are judged. For a full decade, Barry was the undisputed King of the Mountains, rescuing no fewer than 40 men, women and children from the perils of the snow-covered slopes. His base was the 1000-year-old Hospice of St Bernard, high in the Alps, and when he was killed by an avalanche attempting his 41st rescue, they decided that his great name would live on. The honour of being called 'Barry' now goes to the strongest dog in the Hospice. And few have failed to shoulder that great responsibility. In 1935, the race of Barrys almost came to an end when one of them attacked and killed a young girl. The Hospice was inundated with demands that all their dogs should be destroyed, but a few days later that same dog saved the life of a customs official who had been injured in the mountains. There has been no further talk of destroying these famous dogs.

But just to be on the safe side, American officials recruited another breed for the 1979 pre-Olympic Games in the resort of Lake Placid. A long-haired basset hound called Lucille was kitted out with a tankard of refreshment and a back-pack of medical supplies – but, alas, the call for action never came.

Some dogs achieve fame by exercising some sort of sixth sense to alert their owners to approaching disaster. Police dog-handler, Johann Steiner, watched from a window of his house near the Austrian village of Baldramsdorf, as a massive thunderstorm broke over the surrounding mountains. The *Sunday Express* reported that as the lightning flashed, he noticed that his dog Gundo, a seven-year-old Alsatian, had not taken

Lucille, an Olympic qualifier at Lake Placid.

shelter in his kennel, but was pacing to and fro, whimpering and occasionally pawing at the wire fence surrounding his run. Suddenly, as he watched, Gundo took a run at the fence, leapt over the top, ran full pelt for the house and jumped in a window. Johann simply thought his dog was scared of the storm. But, strangely, Gundo appeared to want to go outside again. He carried on whimpering, running between Johann and his parents and the front door. To pacify the excited animal Johann opened the door, and Gundo dashed out, barking and looking up at the mountain that towered above the house. Johann followed him

Gundo took a run at the fence, leapt over the top, ran full pelt for the house and jumped in a window.

and, above the noise of the storm, heard the rumble of rocks and the cracks of breaking trees. To his horror, he realised that a mud slide had started high up the mountain, and was heading straight for his house. Johann rushed his parents and Gundo into the car, and accelerated off into the night. A few hundred yards down the road they stopped in time to see their house crumple and disappear under a 20-foot moving wall of mud. Gundo had got them out just in time.

Not all dogs offer advance warnings of that calibre, but many are pretty good at leaping to the rescue *after* disaster has struck. *Dogs Today* relayed the remarkable experience of Mary Meredith, who slipped while taking a bath, falling forwards and hitting her head on the taps so hard that she knocked herself out, ending up face down in the water. Luckily, as she happened to be alone in the house, she had left the bathroom door slightly ajar. Katie, her flat-coated retriever, who had previously been too frightened of rushing water to go anywhere near the bathroom, sensed Mary was in trouble, and trotted in to investigate. Mary has no idea how long she was unconscious, but when she came round she found that Katie had jumped into the bath, crawled under her chest, and was keeping her head above the water.

Katie had jumped into the bath, crawled under her chest, and was keeping her head above the water.

From Oklahoma comes the story of a stray dog who repaid in a similar way the three-year-old girl who had just taken him in off the streets. The little girl was playing beside a pond with two friends when she slipped and fell in the water. Her two friends ran off to get help, while the dog dived in to try to save her. He didn't have the strength to pull her out, but managed to keep her head above water until the rescuers arrived.

In 1936, *Answers* magazine recorded the story of Bob, a legendary London-born Newfoundland, who saved no fewer than 23 lives before his death in 1874. Bob belonged to a Londoner who used to make frequent trips across the Atlantic to America on business. The dog invariably accompanied his master. On one voyage the ship on which they were travelling was wrecked. There were mighty seas running at the time, and the crew had great difficulty in launching the lifeboats. Bob's master was about to board one of them when he slipped and plunged headlong into the angry seas. Long before the lifeboat had touched the waves, Bob had climbed over the side and disappeared. Two hours later the boats of another vessel, which had rushed to the rescue, came upon a dog and a man clinging to a spar in the water. The man was unconscious, with a nasty scar on his forehead. But the dog, although exhausted, had hold of his coat shoulder in a vice-like grip. The dog was Bob, and the man his master! Incredible though it sounds, this man was shipwrecked a second time on the same journey – but this time, Bob was the only survivor. He came back to London, where he wandered about for some time as a stray. People were falling into the Thames, some by accident, some through intention, then as now. But several were pulled out by a huge hound – a

A dirty, ill-fed dog, but one of amazing strength, skill and friendliness.

dirty, ill-fed dog, but one of amazing strength, skill and friendliness. Naturally, the animal's exploits attracted a good deal of attention. It was Bob, up to his old tricks. He was given a gold medal by the Royal Humane Society, a home, food and a free hand with his rescue work. His life-saving record shows the use he made of his opportunities. He was a real hero.'

Yes, well... ho, hum... maybe the headline should have read 'BRAVE DOG IS VICTIM OF JOURNALISTIC LICENCE'! Then again, perhaps the story *wasn't* over-egged, and that remarkable chain of canine happenings proved that life really was stranger than fiction back in the 1870s.

Swansea Jack with his proud owner and one of his many awards.

Not even a whisker of doubt clouded the achievements of Swansea Jack, a black retriever who saved 29 people and two other dogs from drowning back in the 1930s. Owned by William Thomas of Treboeth, his heroism won him innumerable cups, medals and other mementos, before he was tragically killed by rat poison at the age of seven.

Few dogs make such a habit of rescues from river and sea, but there seems to be no end to the number of dogs with a single great act of heroism in them. Half a century on, the *Daily Mail* chronicled one beneath the headline 'DOG PULLS PC FROM JAWS OF DEATH'. 53-year-old policeman Colin Perks and his loyal Alsatian, Rebel, were chasing three youths through the icy, fast-flowing River Dane at Eaton in Cheshire, when the constable lost his footing and went under. He struggled towards the bank, but weighed down by his uniform and Wellingtons, was unable to keep his head above water. One great rescue later, PC Perks was giving evidence on behalf of the dog who well and truly 'felt his collar': ' The next thing I remember was Rebel grabbing my collar in his mouth and dragging me to the side. Without him, I don't know how I would have got out of the river. I was exhausted, and in danger of becoming hypothermic'. And the officer, just six months away from collecting his pension after 30 years police service,

The Rascal who became a hero.

hinted at a possible canine ulterior motive. 'He is the best dog I have ever had. Thanks to him, we'll be able to enjoy our retirement together.'

Champion sheepdog, Colkington Blue Rascal, didn't hesitate when confronted in 1957 with the thing dogs probably fear most – fire. His owner, 58-year-old French polisher Frank Ashley, had been grooming Rascal in the garden of his North London home when he noticed some earwigs, and traced them to a nest under a pile of wood. He tried to set fire to the nest, but, when it wouldn't catch, tried to give it a little help by pouring on some French polish. Flames leapt up the tin, which exploded in his

Suddenly he found Rascal rolling on top of him.

hands, showering him with burning polish. His shirt and trousers caught alight and he rolled on the ground to try and put them out. Suddenly he found Rascal rolling on top of him to try to help – and Mr Ashley was in no doubt that the dog had saved his life. As the French polisher was lying in hospital being treated for burns, there came the good news that Rascal had survived unscathed – and could still be entered for the Old English sheepdog show the next day as planned.

Nipper, the collie who braved the flames.

In 1985, a five-year-old collie called Nipper won the animal world's equivalent of the Victoria Cross by repeatedly risking his own life to rescue livestock from a blazing barn at Anstey in Sussex. Despite burning his paws, he dashed through the flames time and time again to drive out all but nine of the 370 ewes, lambs, cows and calves trapped in the barn. His reward was a plaque citing 'intelligence and courage, normally awarded to *people* who save the lives of animals'.

In Boston, Massachusetts, they still remember the day, more than half a century ago, when an apartment building caught fire, and men, women and children stumbled, half-dressed, into the street, with the pungent smoke in their

nostrils and the crackle of the spreading flames behind them. A newspaper of the day wrote of 'a blind man, led to safety by his sheepdog, Bruce, who guided him by the trouser leg. Then, as firemen ran out their hoses, out from the now blazing inferno stumbled a woman, mother of an upstairs family. Two small children clung to her arms – yet, letting them go as soon as they were clear of the house, she made as if to turn back herself. Firemen stopped her. Struggling frantically, her face transfixed with terror and anguish, the woman screamed "My baby!" Her youngest child – momentarily forgotten in the first terrified scramble – was trapped inside. There seemed no hope of saving the infant. But Bruce, urged on by his master, aware, like everyone else, of the child's awful fate, dashed to the rescue. The sheepdog emerged just two minutes later. His coat was aflame. He was suffering agonies from burns, particularly around the right eye, which subsequently he lost – but the baby hung in its tiny nightgown from his teeth, miraculously alive and unhurt.'

Water, fire – and now freezing cold. There are dogs to take on all the elements. More than 500 people turned out in temperatures twelve degrees below zero to search for a three-year-old boy missing in woods at Mount Airy, North Carolina. Robbie Campbell, wearing only light play clothes, had been last seen with three of his puppies chasing his grandad's dog. The searchers combed the woods all night, and eventually found Robbie with the three puppies wrapped around him. One had nuzzled under his head, the other two were spread out on top of him. 'He looked as though he was snuggled inside a fur blanket,' said his mother Debra. Later, recovering in hospital from hypothermia, Robbie described how the pups – part German shepherd and part collie, and only twelve weeks old – had rubbed themselves up close to him when he lay down. Doctors confirmed that, with his body temperature down from 98.4 to 94 degrees, the pets had unquestionably saved his life.

It wasn't quite so cold when Alphonse Marie collapsed with a stroke while taking his three dogs for an evening walk in the French port of Boulogne. The pensioner would have frozen to death without the strength, determination and love of his animals – a Labrador, a retriever and a cocker spaniel. Together, the dogs dragged the old man back home by pulling his clothes with their teeth. And, when his son arrived at 6.30 the following morning, he found the dogs huddled round his unconscious father, trying to keep him warm with their bodies – and the Labrador howling for attention.

But the love between dog and master or mistress is a two-way traffic that can stir the deepest soul. When 68-year-old Frank Mattingley lay in a coma in a Southampton hospital, he occasionally muttered the name of his collie, Tipper. Doctors thought it wouldn't do any harm if Tipper was brought along to say goodbye to his master from outside the window of the ward. The dog let out a sad yelp on seeing his master and, deep in his coma, Frank stirred. Nurses wheeled him, still attached to his life-support machine, to the hospital window to see his old friend. And from that moment on, Frank made an amazing recovery.

Nurses wheeled him to the hospital window to see his old friend.

The Bounce Superdogs competition, in aid of the National Canine Defence League, produces hundreds of entries, from which are selected a dozen winners. Amongst the 1991 pack was Meg, a corgi from Neston in Cheshire, who raised the alarm when her owner, Esther Parsons, collapsed unconscious with an undiagnosed duodenal ulcer in the early hours of the morning. Mrs Parsons told how she had just gone downstairs for a drink when she blacked out in the hallway, and somehow fell against the kitchen door handle which fortunately opened the door. She thought this was the only way Meg could have got out of the kitchen – enabling the dog to run upstairs and wake Mr Parsons, who was unable to hear without his hearing aid. Mrs Parsons was rushed to hospital where she made an excellent recovery, but doctors said that if it hadn't been for Meg's prompt action, she might have died.

A later winner of the award was Hanna, a Doberman bitch who chased one of two gunmen who robbed the Cheeky Chappie public house in Brixton in 1974. She was shot twice, and had to have one of her front legs amputated.

While one-off incidents of canine bravery are relatively plentiful, there can be few dogs that display as rich a combination of devotion and skill as Abdul, an eleven-year-old Labrador retriever. After ten years looking after his quadriplegic mistress,

Actresses Sally Thomsett (left) and Yootha Joyce (right) present Hanna with a Bounce Superdog award in 1974.

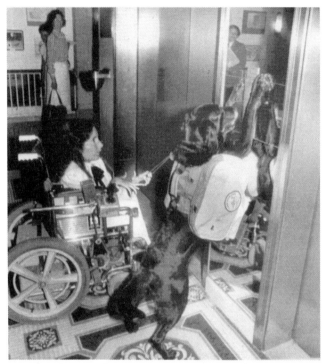

*Going up...
Abdul operates
the lift.*

Kerrill Knaus, in Cotati, California, he had learnt to obey no fewer than 100 commands – including pushing the right elevator button. Hardly surprising then that he won the first annual Animal Assistance Award presented by the American Animal Hospital Association in Boston in 1986.

Lief Rongemo was quietly busying himself around his sixth-floor flat at Malmo in Sweden when, to his horror, he saw his two-year-old daughter crawling along an outside ledge. Following her was the family's pet Alsatian, Roy. While his wife phoned the fire brigade, Lief and a neighbour rushed downstairs with a blanket, which they held out in case the little girl fell. But, before the firemen could push their ladder into position, Roy made his move. He grabbed the girl's clothing with his teeth and gently retraced their steps to the window, where Mr Rongemo pulled them both to safety.

The bravest dog in Britain in 1956 took one look at the cocktail party in her honour at London's Waldorf Hotel – and promptly hid behind her owner's legs. Fly, a border collie, more at home on a remote hill farm in Montgomeryshire, had shown no such reticence when an enraged bull attacked her master, 68-year-old Tom Powell. Fly, who was tending her three-day-old pups at the time, snapped repeatedly at the bull, and finally made it back away by leaping at its nose. The exploit earned her a

He had learnt to obey no fewer than 100 commands – including pushing the right elevator button.

silver cup from the National Association of Dog Biscuit Manufacturers, an inscribed collar, and – most important of all – a giant dog biscuit weighing 23 pounds. But even that didn't tempt Fly out from behind the trousers!

In the Austrian Alps in 1956, a dog clinging to trousers actually saved the wearer's life. The Vienna Society for the Protection of Animals records amongst its medal winners an alert German smooth-haired hunting dog called Brahma, whose uncharacteristic 'worrying of the turn-ups' during a walk through dense fog in the Austrian Alps prevented his master going over the edge of the road into an abyss.

There are hundreds of dogs which have saved one life, but few that can claim to have saved 91 lives all at once. It happened near the turn of the century when the Canadian coastal steamer Ethie ran onto submerged rocks off Martin's Point, Newfoundland. With a tremendous surf breaking over the ship, rescue boats were unable to reach her, and efforts to shoot a line over the rail failed because of the fury of the gale. But on board was a Newfoundland dog. The crew put him over the side with a light line, and – holding it between his teeth – he fought his way through the breakers to the shore. The entire crew was saved, and a few hours later the Ethie was matchwood.

There is no record of precisely how many lives were saved by a cross-bred retriever belonging to a signalman on the Lehigh Valley line in the early days of the railways. The signalman had

Fly, overawed by the big occasion in her honour.

gone out with his red flag to stop an approaching passenger train because he had heard that a culvert further along the line had been washed out. In his excitement he ran too hard and suddenly collapsed with a heart attack. The retriever seized the red flag between his teeth and stood between the rails. The train driver, coming round a curve, saw him and stopped the train in time.

Dogs did invaluable work during the First World War, not just by warning sentries of the approaching enemy, but by finding wounded soldiers in the maze of mud and trenches that formed the long battlefront. The Germans had

The retriever seized the red flag between his teeth and stood between the rails.

20,000 war dogs, while the Russians and the French mustered about 18,000 each. Britain's force was described as 'smaller, but very efficient!' And its greatest hero was Bing. Time and again he warned his battalion of gas – on one occasion detecting it when it had been released six miles away. When they lost count of the lives he had saved, Bing was rewarded with the distinction of becoming the only dog to be decorated for his services during that long war. And, when he died at a ripe old age in 1930, he was buried with full military honours.

An equal amount of military respect was earned by a terrier named Rats, who 'adopted' the soldiers posted to an army base in Northern Ireland during the late 1970s. He achieved television fame when filmed accompanying the troops on a helicopter mission into the 'bandit' country of South Armagh

Rats on helicopter patrol in Northern Ireland.

– an unusual exploit which, for a while, produced two sackfuls of fan mail a day. That was but a drop in the ocean compared to the appreciation he won from the soldiers. On several occasions when out with a foot patrol he detected bombs – one in a booby-trapped lamp-post.

Another dog just thirsting for a place in the newspapers was the Alsatian growling menacingly at the side of PC Michael Parker as he rounded up two burglary suspects in North London in 1984. As the men cowered from the seemingly ferocious beast, the policeman made his trouble-free arrest – and then revealed that the animal was not a trained police dog, but a stray that just happened to have followed him from the police station. When last seen, the Alsatian was being closely questioned in Battersea Dogs Home: 'So – you'd wanted to be a police dog ever since you were a pup? A likely story...'

A DOG'S BEST FRIEND

Cat – what cat? Labrador trainees display their well -tutored indifference. Bottom Tammy also overcomes her natural prejudices.

The Labradors being trained to guide blind people didn't give a second glance as Mischief the Persian cat settled in their midst. Clearly a no-nonsense sort of a creature, she was well used to being a dogsbody. Despite her name, Mischief's job was to bring out the best in the dogs - to make sure they didn't turn a hair when any cat strolled their way. Her presence at regular intervals during their training ensured that when the dogs started guiding blind people, they wouldn't be diverted by passing cats. Mischief started work as a kitten at the Princess Alexandra Guide Dog Training Centre at Forfar in Scotland and, by February 1973, had helped train more than 300 guide dogs. The Centre's boss, Bob Forrester, said: 'It's important that our dogs don't give cats a second look. Mischief does a good job - the dogs don't turn a hair when she's there'.

In 1970, Tammy the 13-year-old Yorkshire terrier went even further. She overcame her natural instincts to mother six Siamese kittens, orphaned when they were just ten days old. Tammy's last pup had died, but her milk came back to feed the kittens. The animals' owner, Marjorie Stead of Higherford in Lancashire couldn't believe it: 'Tammy hates cats, she always chases them out of the garden'.

But even dogs who've got used

to cats have their limits. Wooster, an 11-year-old cross-bred Dalmatian, had got pretty used to her companions at the Cats Protection League shelter at Haslemere in Surrey. But she drew the line at sharing her bone with them, and quickly saw off some adventurous moggies for whom familiarity really had bred contempt.

Wooster defends her bone.

In 1972, Alfred Beautour, keeper at the Amar Circus in Paris, was worried when Nelly the leopard rejected her three newborn cubs. But not for long. Alfred hit on the idea of providing a foster-mother, in the shape of Deesse, an eight-year-old mongrel bitch. She went along with the plan - even if, at first, she did require the reassurance of a comforting human hand as these beasts of the jungle snuggled down for their first feed.

Zoos are never slow to draft in canine foster parents, who seem to take it all in their stride. A black collie, Bessie, is remembered for the way she took to three tiger cubs, fattening them up from one to six pounds in time for their first public outing at London Zoo. And Mr Chips the dachshund stepped up to help another tiger cub rejected by her mother at Southport Exotic Cats Park. Obviously, he couldn't be of much help when

Paternal care from Mr Chips.

it came to feeding, but he proved a dab hand at cleaning up the little furry one afterwards.

Two more unlikely bedfellows were Sanguine Saffron the bloodhound and Micky the tame mouse. They became very close buddies at Plymouth Zoo in 1967, and were even seen chasing each other about the place. As winter came

Micky took to snuggling up to the dog for extra warmth. Saffron treated him extremely gently - presumably because with a face as mournful as his, he needed all the friends he could get.

Just as unlikely was the friendship of a rabbit which strayed into a house on the outskirts of London in 1950, only to be adopted by a cross-bred Dalmatian that lived there. The two became inseparable. Just like Queenie and Thumper, whose life together began in August 1969 when Peter Gibson, of Stakeford in Northumberland, took the family Labrador Queenie and her pup Goldie out into the fields near their home. Goldie found a tiny leveret, and seemed set on a kill. But Queenie's mothering instinct was working overtime. She stepped in to take possession of the leveret and trotted home with it in her soft mouth. The leveret, subsequently named Thumper, was undamaged and apparently unafraid of this new giant creature in her life. Thumper was brought up by Queenie, quickly adapted to eating dog-food, and even when allowed out into the fields again made it plain she preferred a dog's life to that of the wide open spaces from which she came.

Roxanne the Rottweiler made quite a name for herself as a nanny - helping to bring up 15 baby goats on a farm at Warningcamp in Sussex.

With a face as mournful as his, he needed all the friends he could get.

While Sue, an 18-month-old Belgian shepherd, adopted Flossie the lamb when her natural mother ran out of milk. The unlikely pairing saved farmworker Alison Sleightholm the trouble of hand-feeding Flossie, and proved that sheepdogs don't just round up sheep - sometimes they bring them up too.

On a farm near Carlisle, Pud the collie managed to be the proud mother of three puppies and two piglets. Her puppies arrived at the same time as the sow next door gave birth to 18 piglets. Two of the piglets decided they were getting short-changed, and moved across to Pud. Their  owner, Connie Johnston, said: 'We thought at first that the piglets wouldn't survive, but when we put them in with Pud it was love at first sight. She suckles them with the pups, and they play games together. I'm sure they don't notice the difference. In fact the piglets often try to sit up like a dog - and usually fall over. We shall probably end up with grunting dogs and barking pigs'. And lest that should be thought a unique liaison, a French farmer at La Roche D'Abeille has produced a photograph of his sheepdog, Coquette, happily suckling two orphaned piglets after losing her litter of puppies at birth.

Pigs in clover - Coquette with her foster children.

When a forester carried home two exhausted baby deer, whose mother had been frightened away by poachers, they willingly accepted the bottle of babies' milk. That was hardly surprising. Less understandable was the attitude of the forester's pointer, Diana, who quickly assumed the role of nurse. Diana would go to the kitchen asking for the milk bottle, and would then carry it in her jaws to her protegées, holding it there for them to suckle.

Sheepdogs don't just round up sheep.

If the bottle was too high, she would drop her head or change the angle to make it more accessible, and would

carry on doing that until the fawns were satisfied. They became inseparable - so much so that Diana would escort them for walks in the woods. The deer always came back to the house, while Diana seemed to have lost all her hunting instincts and trebled her motherly ones.

A dog may be a man's best friend - but in 1975 a Doberman Pinscher ranked pretty high on at least one bird's list too. The Jesse family of Shelby Township, Michigan, nursed a robin back to health after a storm deposited it on their doorstep. When the bird recovered, it decided that it liked the comforts of the Jesse household rather better than the great outdoors - especially when the family's pet Doberman was around to provide a convenient resting place.

Above Diana – no longer the huntress.
Right 'This does nothing for my image' seems to be the conclusion of a self-conscious Doberman.

Another couple of unusual bedfellows were the dog and the cockerel who settled down side by side each night in the dog's kennel at Henley-on-Thames in 1961. That was just straight-forward friendship.

30 years later came the unusual case of a two-year-old bantam hen that took a pair of new-born Jack Russell puppies under her wing. The dog's mother seemed more than happy to feed them - and then let the hen take over. Worcester farmer Tom Savage said he had never seen

anything quite like it.

Neither, said farmer Ron Hunt, had he, when he discovered a dog that had been mothered by a broody vixen. Striding across his land near Portsmouth one day in 1989, he heard a whimpering, and blinked in disbelief when he saw a cute collie-cross bolt down a fox hole. Ron and a friend waited for the tiny pup to peek out again -

Unlikely kennel partners in Henley.

and then grabbed her. Martin Hunt of the Chichester and District Dog Society said: 'She was sitting by the fox hole and smelling of fox. It was clear she had been living in the hole and was behaving like a half-

A friend waited for the tiny pup to peek out again.

wild animal. She is remarkably healthy, and the fox had cared for her well and saved her life. He had, he added, known of only one other such case in 26 years.

Clearly dogs have no shortage of friends - or of any ability to make friends - in the far corners of the animal kingdom. Although it must be said that humans have no cause to be jealous - yet.

A confused collie pup emerges from her foxhole.

PAMPERED POOCHES

Zurich, December 1988: a pampered pooch samples the latest for the fashionable canine. It is yet another attempt to fashion man's best friend in his mistress's image, and persuade owners everywhere to roll over and lighten their wallets. The new product being launched is perfume for dogs! 'La Pooch' comes in stylish glass bottles and costs £12 for just over one and a half ounces. Created in Paris, it offers different scents for male and female - of course!

There was no mistaking the pungent aroma that hung around Gyp, a three-year-old mongrel who lived in Middleton in Lancashire in 1957. He positively reeked of tobacco smoke - not just because his master Joe Seville enjoyed a pipe, but because Gyp puffed away on one too! After accompanying Joe to work each day with a gang from the North Western Electricity Board, Gyp would sit on his lap as they both indulged in an evening smoke in the front parlour.

144

In 1949, four-legged patients at the Camberwell clinic of the Canine Defence League were offered treatment with 'the latest sun-ray and ultra-violet ray lamps'. They were presented by a Colonel Holland in memory of his late mother, who had been a great animal lover. The first dogs to try out the new treatment were Pin, an Alsatian who had rickets, and Jicky, a mongrel with a leg injury.

High-tech treatment for Pin and Jicky.

Harry Rose, who ran a gentlemen's clothing store in Westcliff in 1952, developed a useful sideline in 'dogs' togs'. He offered them made-to-measure coats, shaped from old pairs of trousers or skirts. The coats weren't just utilitarian. Many had fur collars, with the dog's name stitched inside in coloured tape, and some even had pockets for a

Some even had pockets for a handkerchief – or for bones.

Poser dog goes out on the town.

handkerchief - or for bones.

History repeated itself in 1986, when a London boutique more accustomed to making clothes for rock stars started selling specially coutured 'dog-about-town' outfits. Rich ladies watched this new line in canine clothing being modelled on (regrettably) the cat-walk, and fell over themselves to order tailored one-offs for their pampered pets. An Old English sheepdog sauntered along to the Hippodrome in London's West End to complement the shaggy coat that nature gave him with a silk waistcoat and trendy shades from the boutique. Needless to say, he made it onto the front page of *Hot Dog*, the fashion magazine for all style-conscious pooches.

Occasionally, though, attempts at trendiness can go horribly wrong. In 1985, a visit to a pet beauty parlour left Shane the collie only half the dog he was. Because of a misunderstanding

Before and after – the sorry story of Shane and a haircut.

his long, flowing coat was shaved almost to the skin. His owner, Colin Webb from Watford in Hertfordshire, was furious: 'All I wanted was a nice trim to keep him cool. Now he looks so strange that even the cat is too frightened to go near him'.

Donna Downes of the Brush Puppy Parlour in Harrow said: 'The dog was brought in by the owner's father. He said "Take it all off" - so we did!'

'He said "Take it all off" – so we did!'

The last three decades have been littered with tales of dogs who ended their days in unrefined luxury after being left substantial sums in their owners' wills. The money - usually destined for charity when the dogs move on to the great kennel in the sky - is to guarantee that their last days, or even years, will be spent in five-star luxury. In 1968, Madeline Arnison's £5,000 legacy to Ben the Lakeland terrier kept him in grilled steak, tripe, farm-fresh milk, his favourite tinned baby foods - and regular rides in his own chauffeur-driver limousine. 20 years later inflation had taken its toll. Victor Nicholls needed to leave £25,000 to ensure that Mark, his Scottish terrier, would continue to enjoy the little luxuries he adored - like tea and biscuits for breakfast every morning.

A Florida lady called Eleanor Ritchey loved dogs so much she had no fewer than 150 of them about the house. And when she died in 1968 she left them a cool £8 million. The will stipulated that only when all 150 had passed away could the money be passed to its final destination - the Auburn University's School of Veterinary Science. By December 1983, the School's bonanza hung on the health of just one elderly, lone survivor, Musketeer, who was so enfeebled that whenever he sneezed he fell over. No-one dared suggest that the good folk of Auburn had anything other than his best interests at heart. But at least they knew that after 15 long years they were close to being just one final sneeze away from that £8 million.

They were close to being just one final sneeze away from that £8 million.

Toby appears less than enthusiastic about the party given in his honour.

It may seem chicken feed by comparison, but, in 1990, Toby the Jack Russell had £5,000 lavished on one single party in his honour. All his pals came along to enjoy the dogs' dinner, including Mr Mole the mongrel and Bouncer the Alsatian. Reporters noted that they 'slurped egg-and-milk cocktails, scoffed prime beef and liver and wolfed a kennel-shaped birthday cake. Bow-tied Toby rode in a Rolls Royce to the blow-out at a Bournemouth nightclub, where he was greeted by the town's deputy mayor, Mrs Jackie Harris, and 150 guests'. Grateful owner Tony Goldberg said he threw the lavish party to reward Toby for saving his life - and explained how the devoted animal's affection had stopped him from killing himself. 'I had a broken romance last year. I was all ready to do the hosepipe-in-the-car bit when Toby looked me in the face and conned me out of it. So I felt I owed him a decent birthday party at the very least.' Suggestions that that was the weakest excuse for a beano heard for many a long year were vigorously denied!

Sir William Black - described during the Sixties as the highest-paid man in British industry - enjoyed the company of a basset hound called Fred.

Fred, however, was in the habit of wandering off from his home at Claygate to Chessington Zoo, where dogs are banned. And Sir William, a director of the zoo, had to send his Rolls Royce to bring him back. Fred must have enjoyed the luxury ride, for his occasional visits to the zoo turned into regular weekly illicit trips - one-way walkies, rounded off with a velvet

Home, James! Fred is once again retrieved from Chessington Zoo.

ride home. With that level of devoted luxury, it was hardly surprising that when Sir William became Lord Black in 1968, he asked for a picture of Fred to be included in his coat of arms.

The request was granted by the College of Arms. Indolence immortalised at last!

Every morning in 1963 - without fail - a chauffeur-driven Daimler eased away from a Georgian house in Reading and headed towards open country. Stopping in a quiet lane, the chauffeur stepped out to open a rear door for the owner, Miss Lisa Gray. And that is where the picture of dignity and graceful affluence came to an abrupt halt. For, as Miss Gray descended from the car, she would be almost swept of her feet by a torrent of Pekingese. Like a tan-coloured river in flood, the 30 Pekes flowed from the open door towards the nearest trees for their hour's exercise. Miss Gray, a breeder of some repute, whose dogs seldom sold for below £500, smiled tolerantly and confessed: 'The dogs love riding in high-powered cars. My friends sometimes take them for rides in Rolls Royces, Jaguars and Bentleys, and they get quite excited at high speeds'. Although

30 Pekes flowed from the open door towards the nearest trees.

her chauffeur and kennel manager were on hand to round up the dogs, Miss Gray was often seen plunging into undergrowth herself to gather up the stragglers. As the last Peke was deposited on the back seat, smartly-dressed Miss Gray inspected her laddered stockings and mud-covered shoes. 'Brand new', she said, 'both stockings and shoes. Never mind, it's worth it to keep the little ones happy. Home, please, Ralph.'

Some dogs, however, don't need pampering - they are more than capable of looking after themselves. A prime example was Millie, the White House springer spaniel, who reported a healthy income of $900,000 (just over half a million pounds) - more than four times the salary of her master, President George Bush. It was all down to the runaway commercial success of *Millie's Book*, 141 pages of reminiscences which the clever dog dictated to the President's wife, Barbara. Described as 'an under-the-table look at life in the Bush family', it hovered for around 20

weeks near the top of 1991's bestseller lists, its 400,000 sales dramatically outstripping those of Mr Bush's own biography, *Looking Forward*, which earned a paltry $2,700. Said Marlin Fitzwater, the White House press spokesman: 'This is somewhat embarrassing, but the President is taking it very well'.

Miss Gray's Pekes head for the trees.

The Times had the final word: 'Though dog-lovers and children were the main intended customers for *Millie's Book*, it has become essential reading for political operators and academics who subscribe to Kafka's view that all knowledge, the totality of all questions and answers, is contained in the dog'.

'The President is taking it very well.'

And the money? That went to a charity set up by the First Lady to promote literacy. Perhaps Millie will write volume two herself!

Author's Acknowledgements

Without dogs and owners this book would not have not have been possible. Nor would it have been possible without the journalists and news editors who reported and printed the stories on which this book is based, not forgetting of course the splendid efforts of numerous photographers who, in many cases, patiently reconstructed events, often regardless of the disposition of their subjects.

I am extremely grateful to Ann Head, to Pippin and to Mike Daines for their help in producing the jacket photograph; and to Paul Cooper, Marie Chung and Barry Yeomans for designing and assembling the book. Thanks also to Graham Nown, Dogs Today and Pet Dogs for providing a number of stories.

I am delighted that the same illustrators who provided cartoons for my earlier *Cats in the News* were willing to contribute to *Dogs in the News* – many thanks for their inspired creations to Hector Breeze, Ian Dicks, David Haldane, John Ireland, Ed McLachlan, Rob Shone and Colin Whittock. Additional thanks to Rob for his line drawings on the jacket.

And it almost goes without saying that none of this would have happened without the patience, cajoling, inspiration and skills of Adrian and Rosemary Stephenson at Lennard Books; and the encouragement and help of Roasalie McFarlane and Hilary Foakes at Little Brown.

Once more at the end of another book, a special thank you to my wife Liz for her tolerance and support – and finally my apologies to my cats Rosie and Bonny for spending so much time this year thinking about dogs.

PICTURE
ACKNOWLEDGEMENTS

The publishers would like to thank the following sources for their permission to reproduce copyright material. Where there is more than one picture on a page the pictures are numbered a, b, c etc from the top of the page and from left to right.
Mary Evans Picture Library: 7, 8, 60.
The Hulton-Deutsch Collection: 9, 10, 40, 43b, 46, 61, 74, 79, 90, 103, 104, 105b, 111a, 111b, 128, 145.
Popperfoto: 15, 18a, 18b, 23a, 23b, 28, 31, 43a, 45, 54a, 54b, 56b, 57b, 58, 59a, 59b, 62, 66a, 66b, 70a, 75, 85, 94a, 94b, 109, 110a, 114, 116, 117a, 117b, 118a, 118b, 119, 120, 121a, 121b, 122a, 123, 124, 125, 129, 134, 135, 138b, 141, 142a.
Syndication International: 11, 12, 13, 14a, 14b, 16, 17, 19, 20, 21, 22, 24, 25a, 25b, 26, 29, 30, 32, 33, 37, 39, 41, 42a, 42b, 44, 48, 49, 50a, 50b, 51, 52a, 52b, 53, 55, 56a, 57a, 63, 64a, 64b, 65a, 65b, 67, 68, 69, 70b, 72a, 72b, 72c, 73a, 73b, 73c, 73d, 77, 78, 80, 81a, 81b, 82a, 82b, 86, 87, 89, 95, 96, 97a, 97b, 99, 102, 105a, 106, 107a, 107b, 108, 110b, 113, 115, 122b, 130, 133, 136, 138a, 139a, 139b, 142b, 143a, 143b, 146a, 146b, 146c, 148, 149, 151.